Thank you for purchasing:

Financial and Administrative Policies and Procedures and Other Essentials for the Not-For-Profit Organization – 4th Edition

As a token of our appreciation, we would like to provide you with a soft copy of our manual in order to facilitate the incorporation of its content into your organization's Policies and Procedures.

Please visit our website at: **http://www.SiliconSurfers.com/PubPlus** and complete the request form so that we can email your copy of the manual in Microsoft Word (2003 version) format.

Please keep in mind that this file is provided to you as a courtesy. Please respect our copyright and only make such copies as are required by **your organization alone**.

Sincerely,

AF712451

Gary J. Scapinello, BA, CMA
President, Publications Plus

Section I

FINANCIAL AND ADMINISTRATIVE POLICIES AND PROCEDURES

INTRODUCTION TO FINANCIAL AND ADMINISTRATIVE POLICIES AND PROCEDURES

The Policies and Procedures we have compiled are only meant to act as a starting point. Each Organization should review and modify the material, as necessary, so that they best reflect the intentions and philosophies of their own Boards and the everyday practices of their staff.

The information reported has been gathered from a number of diverse sources and edited to provide a consistent easy reading document. The format we selected best suited our needs but there is no right way or wrong way to write a Policy and Procedure.

Keep in mind that a well-written Financial Policy and Procedure expresses the wishes of the Board and establishes broad guidelines under which the Organization ought to operate. A Financial Policy and Procedure is not intended to provide a great amount of detail but rather it is intended to provide direction.

Helpful Hints:

- The Finance Committee should write the Organization's Financial Policies and Procedures.
- The Board of Directors should approve all Policies and Procedures.
- The Organization's Financial Policies and Procedures should be reviewed annually by the Finance Committee.
- Financial and Administrative Policies and Procedures should be flexible enough so that the day to day operations of the Organization are not impeded, but sufficiently restrictive, so that the financial direction of the Board is followed.

TABLE OF CONTENTS

ACCESS TO DONOR INFORMATION

Effective Date:
Cancels:
Dated:
Signature:
Position:

PREAMBLE

The Fundraising Coordinator is responsible for updating and safeguarding the Organization's donor database. This includes determining what type of information needs to be kept, how it will be used, and who will be allowed access to it.

POLICY

AUTHORIZED USERS

There are three user groups that may have access to the Organization's donor database mailing addresses. These groups are:

1. The Fundraising Committee
2. The Administrative units of the Organization and,
3. Selected external Organizations.

CONDITIONS

The Fundraising Coordinator may provide access to the donor database information subject to the following conditions:

(a) Purpose

The user must inform the Fundraising Coordinator in writing, why the information is being sought. Requests for information must be made not less than five days before the information is required. A sample of the proposed mailing may also be required before approval is granted. The final decision to release donor database information rests with the Fundraising Coordinator.

(b) Disclosure to Third Parties

The information received from the Fundraising Coordinator will not be disseminated by the approved user to other groups or individuals who are not directly associated with the approved project. In the case of mailing labels supplied to a third party as an agent of the user, that agent will also be required to abide by these conditions.

(c) Data Corrections and Update

The user agrees to provide to the Organization information to correct or update individual records. This would include such particulars as place of residence, occupation, job title, and employer's address.

(d) Data Retention

The data provided to the user will remain the property of the Organization and is returnable upon request. Furthermore, individuals, groups or Organizations that have been provided information will not establish an independent database with this information.

PENALTIES

An approved user, or a representative of an approved user, who violates any of these conditions may be denied subsequent access to information. In the case of a flagrant violation, such as the sale of mailing lists to outside parties, the Organization will have recourse to legal action.

DATA ACCESS RESTRICTIONS

Data released to users will be restricted as defined below:

(a) Confidentiality of Giving Records

All individual Giving Records maintained by the Organization are classified as confidential and will not be released without the approval of the donor, or as required by law, or as may be released on a confidential basis to fundraising officers or campaign leaders in the course of their duties. Publication of bequests and other donations that are a matter of public record are excluded from this restriction. The Organization may also release donor-gift statistics in a non-nominative format.

(b) Restrictions on Supplementary Data

Specific information maintained in the database at the request of a particular donor will not be released to other users without the written permission of the donor providing that specific information.

(c) Ordering

Listings, labels or other data must be requested from the Fundraising Coordinator on a Donor Database Request Form.[1] A negotiated charge will apply to requests that involve large listings and/or the production of labels.

[1] See Appendix A.

...Continued

Appendix A

ORGANIZATION'S NAME
Donor Database Request Form

Date of Request: ____________________

Name: ____________________

Address: ____________________

Phone Number: ____________________

TYPE OF INFORMATION REQUESTED

____ List of all Donors
____ List of Donors who have donated within last twelve months
____ List of Organization's Members
____ Other Type of Information Requested - please specify

TYPE OF DATA REQUIRED

Listing to Include:

____ Name
____ Home Address
____ Business Occupation
____ Business Address
____ Home Telephone Number
____ Business Telephone Number

Order of Listing:

____ Alphabetic
____ Postal Code
____ Geographic

If requesting mailing labels please attach a sample of the material to be mailed.

Special instructions or comments:

Signature of requester: ____________________

Please complete and return to:

ACCOUNTING PRACTICES

Effective Date:
Cancels:
Dated:
Signature:
Position:

PURPOSE

To provide general guidelines for reporting and reconciling revenue and expense accounts.

POLICY

Invoices will be paid and revenues will be deposited in a timely manner. Bank and investment accounts and donation receipts will be reconciled at the end of each month.

PROCEDURE

1. To take advantage of discounts and to avoid penalty and/or interest, charges all payments will be made on a timely basis.

2. The Finance/Administration Coordinator will keep a current and detailed record of all receipts and expenditures. All statements received from banks and other financial institutions will be reconciled on a monthly basis.

3. The check number and the date of payment will be recorded on each invoice when paid. The invoice will then be filed in the appropriate vender file.

4. All funds received will be deposited in a timely manner.

5. A monthly reconciliation of balance sheet accounts will be prepared and approved by the Finance/Administration Coordinator.

6. Monthly journal entries will be prepared to record investments, interest, wage and other accruals, as necessary. To ensure completeness of month-end financial statements it may be necessary to process journal entries using reasonable estimates.

ACCOUNTING PRACTICES - CONTROL OF REVENUE BY DEPARTMENTS

Effective Date:
Cancels:
Dated:
Signature:
Position:

SCOPE

All units active in selling goods and services and/or receipting revenue.

POLICY

To provide guidelines that safeguard the Organization's cash and assist in its timely and accurate recording. It should be noted that all revenue received in the form of a donation must first be sent to the Organization's Fundraising Officer for valuation, receipting, and acknowledgement.

CASH CONTROL

1. Overnight retention of cash or other negotiable instruments should not exceed five hundred dollars ($500) unless the department has received prior authorization from the Chief Financial Officer. Departments exempted from the five hundred dollar ($500) holding limit will be assigned written limits based on their individual circumstances.

2. The remitting department must verify all deposits received by the Revenue Control Office. Acceptable methods of verification may include daily cash register tapes or adding machine tapes signed by the person responsible for the deposit. A completed Revenue Remittance Voucher (RRV) must also be attached to the tape.

3. It is the responsibility of all departments to ensure that checks are not stale-dated[1] or post-dated, that the body of the check agrees with the figures and that the check is made payable to the Organization. When appropriate, a piece of identification should be used to verify the signature on the check.

4. Revenue should be stored in a secured locked area with one person responsible for its safekeeping. That person should have the key or combination to the locked area.[2] It is understood that these guidelines may not be feasible for small departments. In these situations alternative arrangements should be discussed with the Chief Financial Officer.

---

[1] A check is stale-dated when the date on the check is more than six months old.
[2] A back up key or knowledge of the combination should also be provided to the person's supervisor.

REVENUE REMITTANCE

1. An RRV and a copy of the cash register tape, or an adding machine tape, must accompany all revenue received by the Revenue Control Office for deposit.

2. The RRV will be completed in duplicate by the remitting department. One copy will be provided to the Revenue Control Office and the second copy will remain with the depositor. RRV forms will be numbered sequentially.

3. The amount deposited must be clearly listed on the RRV along with the appropriate credit coding. Individuals preparing an RRV should sign, or initial the form, and provide their telephone extension or email address so that they can be contacted directly should there be a problem with the remittance.

4. The RRV must also report the amount of Tax that is included in the deposit. When the Tax box on the RRV is left blank, the phrase **EXEMPT FROM TAX** should be written on the face of the form, and a written explanation should be provided. RRV forms received by the Revenue Control Office with no Tax indicated, and with no written explanation, may be returned to the remitting department.

5. If an RRV has a cash component, the remittance must be made in person. To protect the depositor and the staff of the Revenue Control Office such cash deposits will be counted in the presence of the person responsible for completing the RRV.

6. To protect the physical well being of an individual delivering a deposit of greater than five hundred dollars ($500), the depositor must be escorted by a second individual.

7. There must be a separate RRV for each type of currency remitted.

REVENUE CONTROL OFFICE

1. Revenue Control will verify that the amount of the deposit reported by the RRV is in agreement with the cash, checks and other suitable instruments of payment. He/she will then verify that the sales tapes or the adding machine tapes support the deposit.

2. Revenue Control will ensure that the Tax reported by the RRV is reasonable, and that if the Tax box is left blank, an appropriate written explanation is attached.

3. Revenue control will maintain copies of all revenue vouchers and their supporting documents. Such vouchers and documents will be stored for no less than seven years, in a secured area, and will be organized in such a way as to provide for easy access.

4. Revenue Control will be responsible to verify the continuity of the sequential numbering of RRV forms.

ACCOUNTING PRACTICES - FINANCIAL RECEIPTS AND DISBURSEMENTS

Effective Date:
Cancels:
Dated:
Signature:
Position:

POLICY

To provide general guidelines for reporting revenues and expenses, selecting signing authorities, establishing check signing requirements and issuing and maintaining tax receipts.

PROCEDURE

1. The Office Administrator will keep an up-to-date and detailed record of all receipts and expenditures. As part of this process all statements received from banks and other financial institutions will be reconciled on a monthly basis.

2. The check number and the date of payment will be recorded on each invoice when paid. The invoice will then be filed in the appropriate vendor, month or object file.

3. All monies received will be deposited weekly unless the amount on hand exceeds two hundred and fifty dollars ($250). When the balance on hand exceeds two hundred and fifty dollars $(250), a deposit will be made at the end of that working day.

4. The Board of Directors will approve signing authorities for the Organization at a meeting that will be convened immediately following the Organization's Annual General Meeting (AGM). At that meeting sample signatures of the newly authorized signing Officers will be taken and the required forms will be completed and forwarded to the appropriate bank and/or financial institution.

5. Checks drawn on the accounts of the Organization to satisfy unbudgeted expenditures in excess of two hundred and fifty dollars ($250) will require the signatures of two signing Officers. Those signing Officers may include the President, Vice President, Treasurer, Executive Director or any other person approved as a signing Officer by the Board of Directors.

6. A tax receipt will be issued for each donation in excess of twenty dollars ($20). Tax receipts will be issued for lesser amounts if requested by the donor.

7. A reconciliation of donations received and tax receipts issued will be prepared at the end of each month. The Executive Director will review the reconciliation and will sign, or initial the document, as a proof of his/her approval.

8. At the end of each fiscal year the total amount of tax receipted donations must be reported to the Internal Revenue Service. To maintain its charitable status the Organization must file an Annual Information Return within the required time period. Documentation supporting the amount reported by the Annual Information Return will be kept in a safe place for a minimum of seven calendar years from the day that the tax receipt was issued.

AMORTIZATION

Effective Date:
Cancels:
Dated:
Signature:
Position:

SCOPE

All capital assets reported in the ledgers of the Organization (excluding land).

POLICY

All assets acquired through mortgage advances and capitalized will be amortized at a rate equal to the annual mortgage principal payment.[1]

The cost, less any residual value of a capital asset with a limited life, will be amortized over its useful life on a straight-line basis. The Organization will maintain complete and separate accumulated amortization accounts for each significant and meaningful capital asset category. At the minimum the following categories will be required:

(a) Land Improvements	40 years
(b) Buildings	50 years
(c) Furniture and Equipment	10 years

On an annual basis the Finance Committee and the external auditor will review, and amend as necessary, the Organization's policy on amortization. If applicable, the basis of the Organization's policy on amortization will be included in the year-end notes to the audited financial statements.

---

[1] Applicable to only financed assets.

ANNUAL BUDGET

Effective Date:
Cancels:
Dated:
Signature:
Position:

POLICY

A financial budget[1] will be developed prior to the commencement of each fiscal year-end. The budget will be approved by the Board of Directors and will be used to monitor and evaluate the financial status of the Organization throughout the fiscal year. Annual budgets should allow the Organization to meet its goals and successfully carry out its mandate within the community.

PROCEDURE

1. Three months prior to the Organization's fiscal year-end, each committee chair and the Executive Director will complete a preliminary annual budget for their section.

2. Each budget will then be submitted to the Finance Committee where the information will be used to develop a draft-consolidated budget for the upcoming fiscal year.

3. The draft-consolidated budget will then be review at a special meeting of the Board of Directors and amended as necessary. Once amended to the satisfaction of the Board, the budget will be formally approved.

4. Approval of the new consolidated budget will occur not less than one month prior to the Organization's fiscal year-end.

5. On a monthly basis, the Finance Committee will compare actual results with the approved consolidated budget and will advise the Board of Directors of any significant variances. The Finance Committee will also recommend to the Board an action plan that will reduce or reverse significant ongoing negative variances.

6. Midway through the budget cycle the approved consolidated budget will be subject to a formal review by the Board of Directors. The Board will vote on proposed changes to the consolidated budget and if approved they will become part of the official plan.

7. The consolidated budget will conform, as much as possible, to guidelines established by its major funding source.

---

[1] The word "budget" is used interchangeably with the word "plan" and visa versa.

AUTHORIZATION TO COMMIT ORGANIZATION'S FUNDS

Effective Date:
Cancels:
Dated:
Signature:
Position:

PREAMBLE

The Organization's funds are to be allocated in accordance with the Approved Annual Budget. The responsibilities to spend these funds rest with the Directors and Department Heads of the Organization to whom the budget allocations have been made.

PURPOSE

To establish the level of approval required to commit the Organization's funds.

POLICY

The Directors and the Department Heads to whom budget allocations have been made have the authority to commit all of the funds that have been allocated to their department or jurisdictional units, with the exception of commitments restricted by policy, such as personnel.

Directors and Department Heads may delegate signing authority to subordinates. This delegation must be in writing and should specify the type of expenditure that may be approved and the maximum amount that may be committed. Written delegations must be forwarded to the Office Administrator with a specimen signature of the authorized employee. This delegation of authority does not lessen the responsibility of the principle delegate.

When the Organization's policy or procedures require specific levels of approval, authority will not be re-delegated without the written approval of the Executive Director or the Chief Financial Officer.

BEQUESTS AND PLANNED GIVING

Effective Date:
Cancels:
Dated:
Signature:
Position:

SCOPE

The soliciting of all funds, acceptances, releases, and the administration of pledges and bequests.

POLICY

The Fundraising Coordinator will approve all communication with prospective donors. This will ensure that all requests are coordinated, appropriately phrased, and followed up in the most advantageous way.

BEQUEST AND PLANNED GIVING PROGRAM

1. The Fundraising Coordinator is responsible for coordinating, administrating and developing literature that will promote the Bequest and Planned Giving Program of the Organization. This includes liaison, maintaining and safeguarding confidential bequest correspondence, working directly with prospective donors, volunteer leaders, lawyers, estate officers and developing relations with other beneficiaries.

2. All inquiries concerning Bequests or Planned Giving should immediately be brought to the attention of the Fundraising Coordinator. Information received from lawyers, trust companies or executors of estates concerning bequests should also be forwarded to the Fundraising Coordinator. Should legal counsel or execution of releases be necessary the Fundraising Coordinator will refer the matter to the Organization's Executive Director.

3. The Chief Financial Officer of the Organization will be responsible for the execution of releases and other related documents, and the retention of legal counsel. Appropriate Board Members may be consulted and assigned roles.

4. Upon realization of a bequest, the Chief Financial Officer will arrange for an income tax receipt to be issued, if required, and will inform the Executive Director of the terms, conditions and value of the bequest. The value of the asset will also be recorded in the Organization's financial ledgers.

BORROWING POLICY

Effective Date:
Cancels:
Dated:
Signature:
Position:

PURPOSE

To document the authorizations required to borrow funds.

This policy is divided into two sections: operational short-term borrowing and long-term borrowing.

SCOPE

All borrowings including overdrafts, promissory notes, banker's acceptances, leases, mortgages, SWAP transactions, forward rate agreements with Banks and Trust groups, and debentures.

POLICY

This document details the necessary authorizations, limits and requirements to borrow operational and capital funds for the Organization.

Operational Short Term Borrowing

Purpose: Normally these funds will be required as part of the daily cash management activities of the Organization and will be used to bridge the gap between the timing of expenditures and the timing of the receipt of budgeted income.

Terms: It is expected that the term of these commitments will be less than one year. Typically they are 30-90 day transactions. Usually overdrafts, promissory notes, or banker's acceptances are used.

Authorization: The Executive Director, the Chief Financial Officer or the Board elected Treasurer is empowered to authorize transactions under this section. The person responsible for cash management normally carries out such transactions.

Limits: The annual cash flow projections presented as part of the annual budget modified during the year by any subsequent short term financing of approved capital projects and by timing differences, will define the limits in any given year. The Executive Director, the Chief Financial Officer and the Board elected Treasurer will review updates of the Organization's cash position as required.

LONG TERM BORROWING

Purpose: To finance capital projects and capital equipment.

Terms: Terms of the transactions will be for longer than one year. Each project proposal will contain a recommendation on the interest rate and term to maturity of the financing. The instruments chosen may include leases, mortgages, SWAP agreements, Forward Rate agreements, and debentures.

Authorization:

(a) Capital Projects and Capital Equipment of five hundred thousand dollars ($500,000) or less:

The Executive Director is authorized to approve such items that have been identified within the budgeting process and which have received Board of Director approval. The Board of Directors will be informed of this action at their next regularly scheduled meeting.

(b) Capital Projects and Capital Equipment in excess of five hundred thousand dollars ($500,000):

For capital projects and capital equipment in excess of five hundred thousand dollars ($500,000) the Board of Directors' approval is required in advance of the commitment. The Finance Committee will inform the Board of Directors on the financial terms of the proposed transaction. The Executive Director will inform the Board of Directors on the need for the project or the piece of equipment.

Limits: The limit of any transaction will be specific to the individual proposal. Each proposal will include a repayment schedule and the revenue source.

CAPITAL ASSETS AND CAPITALIZATION[1]

Effective Date:
Cancels:
Dated:
Signature:
Position:

SCOPE

All capital assets held by the Organization.

POLICY

On an annual basis the Finance Committee and the external auditor will review and amend, as necessary, the Organization's policy on capitalization. If applicable, the basis of the policy will be included in the Organization's year-end notes to the audited financial statements.

PROCEDURE

Capital assets can be either tangible or intangible[2] properties. To be considered a capital asset all of the following criteria must be met:

(a) the asset must be held for either use in the provision of service, for administrative purposes, for production of goods or for the maintenance, repair, development or construction of other capital assets
(b) the asset must have been acquired, constructed or developed with the intent of being used on a continuing basis
(c) the intent is not to sell the asset in the ordinary course of operations, and
(d) the asset is not held as part of a collection.

The cost of the capital asset to be recorded in the accounts of the Organization will include the amount of consideration given up to acquire, construct, develop, or better an existing capital asset. Moving costs, installation costs and the cost to bring the condition of the asset to the level necessary for its intended use will also be considered part of the capital cost.

The Organization will maintain complete and separate accounts for each significant and meaningful capital asset category. At the minimum the following categories will be maintained:

(a) Land Improvements
(b) Buildings
(c) Furniture and Equipment

The Finance Committee will review all repair, renovation and equipment purchases in excess of five thousand dollars ($5,000) to determine if the cost should be capitalized or expensed. Expenditures less than five thousand dollars ($5,000) will ordinarily be expensed in the year in which they occur.

---

[1] The appropriate section of the CPA (Certified Public Accountants) handbook that covers capital assets should be read by all members of the Finance Committee.

[2] Intangible properties are assets that lack physical substance and include such things as copyrights, patents and software.

CAPITAL ASSETS AND CAPITALIZATION

Effective Date:
Cancels:
Dated:
Signature:
Position:

SCOPE

All capital assets held by the Organization.

POLICY

Capital assets are recorded at cost with the exception of donated assets that are recorded at appraised value. All equipment and improvement to the building either purchased or financed by mortgage advances will be capitalized.

On a regular basis the Finance Committee, the Treasurer, and/or the external auditor will review, and amend as necessary, the Organization's policy on capitalization. If applicable, the basis of the policy will be included in the Organization's year-end notes to the audited financial statements.

CHECK REQUISITION

Effective Date:
Cancels:
Dated:
Signature:
Position:

POLICY

The Board of Directors has established the following procedure for requesting and authorizing payments by check. This policy is designed to control the check writing function and to safeguard the Organization's assets.

PROCEDURE

A check requisition must be completed prior to the issuance of a check. To properly complete a check requisition the following information must be reported:

1. Date - Date of requisition.
2. From - Name of the person requesting the check, including the department and the telephone extension.
3. Pay to - Name and complete address of the payee.
4. Special Delivery Instructions - If the check is not to be directly routed to the payee then the appropriate routing instruction needs to be reported.
5. S.I.N. - If honoraria included in payment.
6. Date Required - Record the date that the check is required.
7. Currency of Payment - U.S., Canadian, or other.
8. Amount - Amount of payment required expressed as $0,000.00.
9. Purpose - Reason for payment cross-referenced to supporting details or documents (attach).
10. Coding Section - The complete account code or codes to be debited.
11. Approved by - Requires authorized signing authority.
12. Bank Account - Include the bank where the check will be drawn (operating account, other).

DISTRIBUTION

All check requisitions are required in duplicate except payments for honoraria. Requisitions for the payment of honoraria are to be completed in triplicate to facilitate the issuance of a *(enter appropriate tax form).*

All copies of completed check requisitions are to be forwarded to the Accounting Department for processing.

...Continued

Responsibility

The Accounting Department is responsible for verifying that the amount requested is supported by the attached documents and that the signature is that of the appropriate authority.

Honoraria

When an honorarium is to be paid to an existing employee, in recognition of special services outside the normal duties of the position, such payment should be made through the Employee Data Form. An accompanying memorandum explaining the nature of the payment, and the period that the honorarium covers, needs to accompany the Data Form. If the special service has been provided to a department, other than the employee's regular department, this fact should be included.

Check requisitions completed for honoraria payments for non-employees should be forwarded to the Human Resources Department together with the relevant supporting documentation.

All honoraria payments require the prior approval of the Board of Directors. Such approval will be recorded in the Board minutes.

CHECK SIGNING AUTHORITY

Effective Date:
Cancels:
Dated:
Signature:
Position:

SCOPE

All checks drawn on the Organization's bank accounts.

POLICY

The Board of Directors is obligated to protect the assets of the Organization. To fulfill this obligation, financial safeguards need to be established and adhered to. This policy establishes these safeguards when checks are drawn from the Organization's accounts.

PROCEDURE

1. The Executive Director may sign his/her own paycheck if one member of the Board of Directors also signs the check. If the paycheck is not the usual amount then the signatures of two Directors is required.

2. The Executive Director will sign his/her own expense check if the amount of the check is less than two hundred and fifty dollars ($250). Any amount greater than that must be signed by two Directors.

3. Any extra monies, such as an honorarium, distributed to any employee must be acknowledged in writing and signed by the Chair of the Human Resources Committee and by one Board member.

COMPANY CREDIT CARDS

Effective Date:
Cancels:
Dated:
Signature:
Position:

SCOPE

All corporate credit cards issued in the name of the Organization.

PURPOSE

To control the use of the Organization's credit card(s).

POLICY

1. Any officer of the Organization may authorize the use of the Organization's credit card.

2. The Finance/Administration Coordinator will process all credit card applications.

3. The Executive Director will approve all credit card application.

4. The Executive Director and the Finance/Administration Coordinator will monitor all credit card use.

5. A copy of all credit card agreements will be kept on file.

6. All credit card purchases must be adequately documented.

7. The Organization's credit cards are not to be used for cash advances or to purchase personal goods or services.

8. In the event that a credit card is lost or stolen the cardholder will immediately report the loss to the appropriate financial institution and to the Finance/Administration Coordinator.

9. To establish the remaining credit on the card, the Finance/Administration Coordinator must be immediately informed of each purchase.

COMPUTER INFORMATION BACK UP

Effective Date:
Cancels:
Dated:
Signature:
Position:

PREAMBLE

The Organization stores critical information and records it on its network file server. This information must be safeguarded against fire, flood or any other harmful act.

SCOPE

All computer data files stored on the Organization's network file server.

POLICY

To safeguard critical data and ensure the continuous operation of the Organization, computer data files will be adequately backed-up on a timely basis.

PROCEDURES

1. Information on the Organization's file server will be backed-up on a daily basis.

2. Ten back-up tapes will be rotated over a two-week period (10 business days) before the first of the ten tapes is reused. The tapes will be labeled consecutively from 1 to 10 with tape 1 being used for Monday, tape 2 for Tuesday, tape 3 for Wednesday, tape 4 for Thursday, tape 5 for Friday, tape 6 for Monday, etc.

3. The integrity of the back up will be confirmed when tape 5 and tape 10 are processed.

4. All back-up tapes will be kept off-site. The Executive Director and/or Finance/Administration Coordinator will bring the appropriate tape on-site daily or on request.

5. A tape back-up will be completed and retained off-site for each quarter – March 31st, June 30th, September 30th and December 31st – and reused the following year.

6. A tape back-up will be completed and retained off-site after completion of the Organization's fiscal year-end.

7. To ensure the integrity of the data being backed-up, any problem with the tape back-up system or tape cartridge will be researched immediately and remedied promptly.

8. The back-up medium should be replaced as per the recommendation of the manufacturer.

COMPUTER USAGE

Effective Date:
Cancels:
Dated:
Signature:
Position:

SCOPE

All users of the computer resource, including all hardware and software, whether owned, leased, rented or on loan to the Organization.

POLICY

All unauthorized or illegitimate use of the system is strictly prohibited. Excessive personal use of the resource is also prohibited, especially when it overburdens the system and impacts on its efficiency. Other prohibited uses include, but are not limited to, the infringement on the intellectual rights of others, unauthorized modification and/or destruction of hardware and software, attempts to circumvent the security system to gain access to unauthorized systems and/or files, interference with the ability of others to access the resource in order to perform their duties, and the use of the Organization's computer resource for personal gain.

It is the responsibility of all users to respect the intellectual property rights of all authors, contributors and publishers, and to protect and safeguard their own password(s) and system(s) from unauthorized users. Furthermore, all users must adhere to the terms and conditions of all software licenses, contracts, agreements and policies which legally bind the Organization to third parties.

All electronic information residing on the Organization's networks and equipment, including electronic email, is the property of the Organization and is subject to examination by authorized staff if any breach of this policy is suspected, or if it is necessary to comply with a federal or state law.

Any employee in violation of this policy may be denied access to the Organization's computer resource and may also be subject to other disciplinary action.

The health and well being of the resource is ultimately the responsibility of its users who must all guard against internal and external disruptions, threats and abuses to the system.

CONFLICT OF INTEREST

Effective Date:
Cancels:
Dated:
Signature:
Position:

PREAMBLE

Occasionally it will be in the best interest of the Organization to acquire goods and services from, or to give or sell goods or services to, external Organizations that are associated with the Organization or with some of its employees. To protect employees of the Organization, as well as the Organization itself, from allegations of a conflict of interest, transactions must be dealt with in an arms-length[1] basis.

SCOPE

This policy includes all Officers, Directors and Employees of the Organization in an executive, professional, administrative, supervisory or technical capacity. It also includes any person responsible for the approval, issuance or allocation of an order, contract, commitment or specification for materials or services to be furnished by external suppliers. Any of the above-mentioned persons, or person, responsible for the determination of prices or terms, for the sale of, or purchase of materials, supplies or services, to clients or from suppliers, on behalf of the Organization also falls under this policy.

POLICY

1. Members[2] of the Organization are prohibited from accepting substantial gifts, benefits or favors for their use or enjoyment offered by a client, supplier, proposed supplier, purchaser, proposed purchaser, donor, proposed donor, association, institution or person with whom the member is dealing with on behalf of the Organization.

2. Members of the Organization must always deal at arms length when conducting business or having financial dealings on behalf of the Organization with any enterprise. In particular:

   (a) the Organization's members are prohibited from approving requisitions or payments for the purchase of goods or services from enterprises in which the member, or some member of his/her immediate family[3] has a financial interest, and
   (b) the Organization's members are prohibited from selling, giving or approving sales or gifts to enterprises in which the member, or some member of his/her immediate family, has a financial interest.

---

[1] An employee will not be dealing at arms length when the Organization is buying, selling or giving goods or services from, or to, that employee, or, from or to some member of his/her immediate family, or, when the Organization is dealing with an enterprise where that employee, or some member of his/her immediate family, has a pecuniary interest.

[2] Members include Officers, Directors and Employees of the Organization.

[3] Immediate family means spouse, common-law spouse, children, parents, in-laws, or relations residing in the same household.

...Continued

3. Members of the Organization are prohibited from doing business with, having financial dealings with or receiving remuneration or substantial[1] gifts from any supplier, purchaser or enterprise that competes or conflicts with the aims and objectives of the Organization.
4. When any member of the Organization finds himself/herself in a situation that breaches, has breached or is likely to breach these guidelines, the member will immediately disclose the matter to his/her immediate supervisor and to the Executive Director. The supervisor will either take over the matter personally or will delegate it to another employee, ensuring in the process that no further breach of this policy occurs. In each case, where a breach of this policy has been reported to a supervisor, the Executive Director will be immediately advised in writing of the breach. Any gift or benefit unknowingly received by an employee must be turned over to the Organization with a disclosure.

---

[1] Substantial means large in amount or of considerable value. In any event, for the purpose of this policy substantial will mean any benefit having a value in excess of one thousand dollars ($1,000).

CONTRACTS - DELEGATION OF AUTHORITY TO SIGN

Effective Date:
Cancels:
Dated:
Signature:
Position:

POLICY

As part of its normal operations the Organization may enter into two types of contracts. One type of contract will commit the Organization to purchase certain services or materials from an outside party. The second type will obligate the Organization to perform a service or to supply materials to an outside party.

This policy provides signing authority guidelines for both types of contracts.

PROCEDURE

DELEGATION

1. The Executive Director or the Office Administrator will normally sign purchase contracts on behalf of the Organization.

2. Construction contracts in excess of twenty thousand dollars ($20,000) will be signed by the Executive Director and the President of the Board of Directors or by any two signing officers of the Organization.

3. Special consideration is needed when the Organization contracts with another party to perform a service, provide advice, information, or supply material, whether or not income is the intent of the partnership. In such situations the Organization must ensure that the legal, financial and insurance implications are thoroughly understood. Typically, all such contracts will be signed on behalf of the Organization even though specific individuals or departments will provide the service.

   The signing authorities for such "performance" contracts will be as follows:

   All contracts, documents or written instruments requiring execution by the Organization will be signed by one signing officer from the Board of Directors and the Secretary of the Board. Once appropriately signed, such contracts, documents or written instruments will bind the Organization without any further authorization or formality. The Corporate seal of the Organization may, when required, be affixed thereto.

   From time to time the Board of Directors may authorize other officers of the Organization to execute contracts, documents or written instruments.

CONTRACTS - GENERAL

Effective Date:
Cancels:
Dated:
Signature:
Position:

SCOPE

All contracts.

POLICY

A contract is an agreement enforced by law that binds two or more parties to do or not to do some defined thing. Each contract entered into by the Organization should maximize the benefit of that agreement and at the same time protect the Organization's good name.

PROCEDURE

1. A minimum of three tenders will be required whenever the financial costs or benefits from a contract is likely to exceed two thousand five hundred dollars ($2,500) or, when the contract will obligate the Organization for a period greater than one calendar year.

2. All contracts entered into by the Organization must be reviewed and approved by the Board of Directors.

3. Two persons who have been granted signing authority by the Board of Directors will sign each contract. Each contract will be witnessed, dated and embossed with the Organization's corporate seal. The Organization will also ensure that a completed copy of the final contract is made available to all other signatories.

4. The original signed contract will be kept in a secure place at the Organization's business office.

CONTRACTS - PURCHASE OF SERVICE

Effective Date:
Cancels:
Dated:
Signature:
Position:

SCOPE

All Purchase of Service contracts.

POLICY

A Purchase of Service contract is a written agreement between the Organization and an outside agency or individual. A Purchase of Service contract helps to ensure that the Organization's funds are expended appropriately and used for the purposes intended. All Purchase of Service contracts must meet the Organization's conflict of interest guidelines.

PROCEDURE

1. At the minimum each Purchase of Service contract entered into by the Organization will provide the following information:

   (a) the nature of the service
   (b) the financial obligations agreed to
   (c) the period of time that the contract covers
   (d) the invoicing procedure, or a payment schedule
   (e) a termination clause
   (f) a table of contents regarding the negotiated work plan
   (g) the staff member or members given the authority to act on behalf of the Organization.

DISPOSAL OF SURPLUS OR OBSOLETE ASSETS

Effective Date:
Cancels:
Dated:
Signature:
Position:

SCOPE

All surplus or obsolete furniture, equipment or materials owned by the Organization including:

1. all furniture, equipment or materials that are additional to the requirements of a department after taking into account the needs of the department over the next two years,

2. all furniture, equipment or materials rendered useless due to normal wear, breakage beyond economical repair, and/or considered valueless for trade-in purposes and,

3. all technically obsolete equipment or materials that have been rendered obsolete due to advances in technology.

POLICY

To establish a procedure that simplifies the identification, declaration and disposal of surplus or obsolete furniture, equipment and materials.

PROCEDURE

DECLARING FURNITURE, EQUIPMENT AND MATERIALS SURPLUS OR OBSOLETE

When furniture, equipment or material becomes surplus or obsolete to a department, the Office Administrator for the department will complete the standard Declaration Form and will then forward it to the Purchasing Department.

A standard Declaration Form should provide the following information:

(a) Date the item was declared surplus or obsolete
(b) The name of the declaring department and its general ledger accounting code
(c) Physical location of the item
(d) Quantity of items being declared (e.g. 6 tables)
(e) Complete description of the item (model, serial number, etc.)
(f) Original value of the item and the year purchased (estimate if not known)
(g) Condition of the item (good, fair, poor, or scrap)
(h) Suggested prospective buyers, if known at the time of declaration
(i) If the item is to be replaced
(j) Signature of department head.

Appraised Value

After discussing the appraised value with the declaring department and with an expert, if required, the Executive Director will establish the final value of the item.

Trade-Ins Of Surplus Or Obsolete Furniture, Equipment Or Materials

When a department needs to replace the item that it has declared obsolete, information concerning the item must be included on the purchase requisition for its replacement. By including this information on the purchase requisition, the Purchasing Department is alerted of a possible "trade-in", which may be of benefit while negotiating the final price of the replacement.

The Purchasing Manager may use the item as a trade-in for another department that is purchasing a similar item if the item is not needed by the declaring department. In any case, the "trade-in" value received will be identified with the declaring department and the appropriate credit will be transferred to it.

Transfer Of Surplus Or Obsolete Furniture, Equipment Or Materials

The Office Administrator of a declaring department will advertise surplus or obsolete furniture, equipment or materials. Items declared must be considered to be acceptable for use by other departments within the Organization. All articles will be transferred on a first come, first serve basis.

Public Sale Of Surplus Or Obsolete Furniture, Equipment Or Materials

Any surplus or obsolete furniture, equipment or materials that are not transferred to another department, or used as "trade-ins", will be offered for sale to the employees of the Organization. If the article is not sold to an employee after ten working days then the article will be publicly advertised for sale.

The methods of sale may include solicited quotations with the item going to the highest bidder, cash and carry, public auction, or any other means deemed appropriate.

Sales made to the general public will be by cash or check made payable to the Organization. Checks will only be accepted when accompanied by appropriate identification. Applicable sales taxes will apply to all articles sold, except when the purchaser submits the necessary proof of exemption certificate. Net proceeds from all cash sales will be credited to the declaring department.

Surplus or obsolete furniture, equipment or materials will be sold as is and without warranty. It will be the responsibility of the purchaser to arrange for the packing and the removal of the purchased goods within three working days following the day of sale.

DISPOSAL OF SURPLUS OR OBSOLETE ASSETS

Effective Date:
Cancels:
Dated:
Signature:
Position:

PURPOSE

It is the purpose of this policy to make surplus furniture, equipment and materials available to other departments before it is presented for sale to the general public or scrapped. By providing the selling department with the proceeds from the sale, there is an incentive for departments to review their furniture, equipment and material holdings and report those which have become surplus.

SCOPE

All furniture, equipment and materials declared surplus or rendered obsolete due to technical advances.

POLICY

1. The Office Administrator is responsible for the storage, reissue and disposal of surplus and obsolete furniture, equipment and materials within his/her own department.

2. All departments will report to their Office Administrator all furniture, equipment and materials that have become surplus to their needs.

3. The Office Administrator will maintain an inventory of all surplus items and provide the Purchasing Department with a copy. The Office Administrator will also establish the value of surplus items. A department requisitioning an article will be asked to inspect the item for acceptability.

4. When a surplus item is sold internally, an Internal Transfer Invoice[1] or journal entry will be used to record the sale's transaction.

5. In cases where the surplus item is not required by the Organization it may be offered for sale to the public. Proceeds from a public sale will be reported as revenue by the Organization. The revenue will be credited to the selling or declaring department, via the accounting code that was provided when the item was declared surplus. The Chief Financial Officer reserves the right to determine the disposition of net proceeds on major items.

6. When items are declared surplus as the result of the Organization being terminated, or vacating its premises, net proceeds from sales to outsiders will be credited to the Organization as a whole and not the declaring department. The Chief Financial Officer and the Executive Director may grant exceptions.

7. Due to the lack of central storage space, it may be necessary to leave certain surplus items in the declaring department until they are sold or disposed of in some other way.

---

[1] This assumes an in-house charge out system.

DISTRIBUTION OF FINANCIAL INFORMATION TO THIRD PARTIES

Effective Date:
Cancels:
Dated:
Signature:
Position:

SCOPE

All financial information, regardless of form, requested by a third party.

POLICY

From time to time the Organization will be requested to supply financial information to a third party. Such a request may help ensure compliance with a license that the Organization is a party to, or may be needed to satisfy the terms of a funding application. In all instances, the Office Administrator, the Executive Director, or the Treasurer must first approve of the distribution of financial information before it is released.

PROCEDURE

1. The employee receiving the request will prepare the financial information in the format requested by the third party.

2. The information should be clearly marked audited or unaudited, as appropriate.

3. The financial information will then be given to the Office Administrator, the Executive Director, or the Treasurer for review and approval. The purpose and the intended use of the requested material and the source of the request should also be made clear.

4. The Office Administrator, the Executive Director, or the Treasurer will authorize distribution of the information by initialing the Organization's pre-printed Request for Information Form.

DONATIONS

Effective Date:
Cancels:
Dated:
Signature:
Position:

SCOPE

All tax receipted donations.

POLICY

Official tax receipts will be issued in accordance with the regulations set out by the Internal Revenue Service. A tax receipt, equivalent to the fair market value of a donated good, will be issued for a gift in kind.

PROCEDURE

1. A permanent record of all gifts donated and accepted by the Organization will be maintained. At the minimum each record will include the date the gift was received, the full name and address of the donor, the nature of the donation, and the number of the tax receipt issued for the donation.

2. A thank you letter will accompany all tax receipts mailed to donors. This formal acknowledgement will be carried out in a timely basis and will not extend beyond five working days from the date that the gift was received.

3. Blank tax receipts will be kept on site and in a secure place. Access to the tax receipts will be restricted to the Office Administrator and the Executive Director.

4. Two signatures will be required on all tax receipts. Signatories will be as authorized by the Board of Directors.

5. All numbered tax receipts must be accounted for. Spoiled tax receipts will be marked void and kept in a secure place for a minimum of seven calendar years from the date of the occurrence. A written report will be required whenever a numbered receipt is missing. The report will include the number of the missing tax receipt, the date that the loss occurred or was discovered and an explanation of the loss. The report will be signed by the Office Administrator, the Executive Director, and by any other employee of the Organization whose name appears in the report.

6. Tax receipts will not be backdated.

7. An Annual Information Return will be completed and filed with the Internal Revenue Service no later than the fifteenth day of the fifth month following the Organization's fiscal year-end. The Annual Information Return will be completed by the Office Administrator and reviewed and signed by the Executive Director and/or Treasurer.

...Continued

8. With the exception of bequests, the Organization prefers that donations not be made anonymously.

As is required by Generally Accepted Accounting Principles (GAAP), donated goods are to be recorded as revenue, with an offsetting expense or asset, as appropriate, in the fiscal year that the donation was received.

DONATIONS - ETHICAL GUIDELINES FOR ACCEPTING

Effective Date:
Cancels:
Dated:
Signature:
Position:

SCOPE

All donations offered to the Organization.

POLICY

The Organization will not knowingly accept donations from corporations, foundations, other Organizations, events or individuals, nor will it participate in or endorse an event, or employ third party fundraisers that are not supportive of its goals. The Organization will not allow product representations of its logo on any corporate sponsorship. Furthermore, the Organization will not allow access to its consumers for promotional media or advertising without the express written consent of the consumer or consumers' parent or guardian *(if applicable)*. In addition, the Organization will not allow open access to its employees for promotional media, advertising, or perceived gain without the express written consent of its Board of Directors.

Companies promoting, producing or selling the following products will not be considered for direct corporate sponsorship: cigarettes, tobacco, or alcohol. The Board of Directors of the Organization will review all donations on a case by case basis for acceptability.

Human Rights

The Organization supports the Human Rights Code Statutes of *(enter appropriate jurisdiction)* and will not knowingly accept funds from, or align itself with, any funding source which is known to have violated the rights of an individual as a result of that person's race, religion, gender, sexual preference or disability.

Criminal Activity

The Organization will not knowingly accept donations from any funding source involved in any criminal activity past or present.

DONATIONS[1] IN KIND - APPRAISALS, RECEIPTS AND RECORDS

Effective Date:
Cancels:
Dated:
Signature:
Position:

SCOPE

Donations in Kind, where the objects donated become the permanent property of the Organization and a tax receipt for value is issued.

POLICY

The Organization periodically receives donations in the form of art, library books, collections, etc. These gifts are referred to as Donations in Kind and usually require evaluation for the purpose of formal acknowledgement and issuance of tax receipts. In keeping with the tax statutes, these tax receipts must be issued in a format acceptable to the Internal Revenue Service. They must also include the Organization's registration number as a registered charitable Organization.

This policy outlines the process that must be followed when the Organization is offered a gift in kind.

PROCEDURE

1. Prior to accepting a Donation in Kind the gift must first be approved by the Executive Director or his/her delegate.

2. When a Donation in Kind has been approved, the Fundraising Coordinator will assist in or complete the negotiations with the donor. When a tax receipt for the value of the donation is issued, the Fundraising Coordinator will also arrange for an appraisal to be made in a manner acceptable to the Internal Revenue Service.

3. The Fundraising Coordinator will issue tax receipts for Donations in Kind. Such tax receipts will report the appraised value of the gift and the name of the appraiser. A copy of the appraisal certificate will be attached to each tax receipt.

4. A record of Donations in Kind will be maintained by the Organization for a period of not less than seven years. At the minimum, the record will include the name of the donor, the latest known address of the donor, the appraised value of the gift, the number of the tax receipt issued, and the date it was issued.

5. When a donor does not require a tax receipt, an acknowledgement of the gift will be issued by the Organization. Letters of acknowledgement will be mailed not more than ten working days after acceptance of the gift. A record of all such donated objects will be maintained with the words "no appraised value" shown opposite them.

---

[1] Also know as a gift in kind.

...Continued

6. Upon receiving a Donation in Kind the Fundraising Coordinator will arrange to have the gift included in the Organization's collection or inventory. The Fundraising Coordinator will also provide the Chief Financial Officer with the necessary information so that the article can be properly recorded into the asset accounts and adequately insured.

DONATIONS IN KIND - APPRAISALS, RECEIPTS AND RECORDS

Effective Date:
Cancels:
Dated:
Signature:
Position:

PREAMBLE

The Organization periodically receives non-cash donations in the form of gifts. These gifts are referred to as donations in kind and usually require evaluation.

SCOPE

All donations in kind.

PURPOSE

The following policy establishes the method to be used to appraise a donation in kind, guidelines for issuing a tax receipt, and the appropriate records that need to be maintained to safeguard the integrity of the Organization and the donor.

POLICY

1. All donations in kind must first be approved by the Executive Director, or designate.

2. When a donation in kind has been approved, a tax receipt for the appraised value of the donation will be issued.

3. An appraised value will be established in a manner acceptable to the Internal Revenue Service.

4. A copy of the appraisal certificate and/or any other supporting documents will be attached to each tax receipt.

5. An item that is to be retained for use by the Organization must be added to the accounts of the Organization and adequately insured.

ELECTRONIC MAIL - email

Effective Date:
Cancels:
Dated:
Signature:
Position:

PREAMBLE

Electronic mail has greatly facilitated the ability to communicate both internally and externally. Unfortunately, this new communications tool also has the potential for misuse. While speaking directly to electronic mail, the principles in this policy are consistent with existing policies that apply to other forms of communications.

Owing to the "newness" of electronic mail as a medium of communications, many legal issues are now being addressed before the courts and legislatures. It is therefore advised to seek legal council once the Organization has a draft set of electronic mail policies.

SCOPE

This policy applies to all users of the Organization's electronic mail resource.

POLICY

The Organization provides electronic mail facilities to support its administrative functions and its service activities. Any use of the electronic mail facility, which may interfere with these functions or harm the reputation of the Organization, is strictly prohibited. In addition, no user of the Organization's electronic mail facility will knowingly conceal or misrepresent their name or affiliation in an email message. Nor will they knowingly alter the source, or the destination, of any address or use the resource for personal gain or to interfere with, degrade, demean or threaten any other individual.

Before using the Organization's email facility an individual must consent to all of the provisions of this policy and must comply with all its terms and conditions. Any user of the Organization's electronic mail system, whose actions violate this policy, may have their email privileges limited, or denied, and may suffer other disciplinary action.

PRIVACY

The Organization cannot guarantee the privacy or confidentially of any email message or document whether sent or received.

While the Organization's electronic mail administrator(s) does not routinely monitor the content of email messages, the Organization does reserve the right to, inspect, copy, store, disclose and/or purge the contents of any email message. However, these actions will be taken as a last resort and only when it is believed that such action will prevent or correct improper use, satisfy a legal claim or insure the proper operation of the resource. Before an email administrator takes any action he/she must first obtain the appropriate administrative authority.

EMERGENCY FINANCIAL LOAN PROGRAM

Effective Date:
Cancels:
Dated:
Signature:
Position:

PREAMBLE

From time to time a consumer may require emergency cash assistance to purchase an assistive device. If funding from the Organization's Assistive Devices Program is not available then the Organization may wish to provide the consumer with a short-term loan.

SCOPE

All of the Organization's consumers requiring emergency cash assistance to help in the purchase of an assistive device.

POLICY

The Organization recognizes the benefits that an Emergency Financial Loan Program brings to its consumers. The Organization also recognizes the inherent liability of operating such a program.

To minimize the risk the following set of guidelines should be followed:

1. Only funds earned by fundraising activities will be made available to the loan pool. All government funds will be excluded from the program.

2. All parties to the loan will agree to all of its terms before any funds are provided. At a minimum, each agreement will include the following information:

   i Consumer's name
   ii Date of the agreement.
   iii Detailed description of why the funds are required
   iv The amount of the Loan (not to exceed $1,000)
   v A repayment schedule (not to exceed 90 calendar days).

   Each loan agreement must be signed by the consumer (or his/her authorized representative), the Financial/Administrative Coordinator and the Executive Director.

3. All parties to the loan will receive a signed copy of the final agreement.

4. Consumers may request more than one loan during a single fiscal year.

5. When possible, the Organization will make the check payable to the product vendor.

ENDOWED FUNDS - GENERAL

Effective Date:
Cancels:
Dated:
Signature:
Position:

SCOPE

General Endowment Fund (GEF).

PURPOSE

To report the guidelines under which the General Endowment Fund will operate.

DESCRIPTION

The General Endowment Fund consists of monies from external non-operating sources, such as a donation. The objective of the Fund is to protect its capital, while at the same time provide a perpetual annual flow of return on investment, which can be used to support a project, or projects, selected by the organization. In general, only the return on investment generated by the Fund during the prior fiscal year may be spent. Under special circumstances, however, the Board may authorize spending GEF capital.

POLICY

1. The Board of Directors has the sole authority to create, dissolve, add to, or deduct from the General Endowment Fund. The Board of Directors is also responsible for updating and approving the Terms and Conditions under which the GEF will operate.

2. To avoid a reduction in real spending power, each year a portion of the income earned by the General Endowment Fund will be returned as capital.

3. Any unspent expendable, or part thereof, created in one fiscal year will be carried forward to the subsequent fiscal year where it once again will be considered expendable.

4. If the amount of the expendable cumulative carry forward becomes excessive, the Board of Directors may agree to return part, or all, of the expendable portion to the GEF as capital. This return of funds not only increases the Endowment's capital base but also the amount of the expendable portion that will be calculated in future years.

5. On an on-going basis the Board will review, update, prioritize, approve budgets, and maintain a list of projects and financial requests eligible to receive GEF support.

6. The Board of Directors may delegate all, or part of the General Endowment Fund's operational functions to a person, or to a committee such as the Executive or Finance Committee. This act of delegation, however, does not absolve the Board from its responsibility regarding the ethical operation of the Fund.

...Continued

7. On a quarterly basis a Statement of Revenue and Expense for the Fund will be presented to the Board at a regularly scheduled meeting.

EXTENSION OF CREDIT AND COLLECTION OF GENERAL RECEIVABLES

Effective Date:
Cancels:
Dated:
Signature:
Position:

PREAMBLE

It is recommended that sales staff encourage the use of cash, check, credit card or debit card when transacting a sale. Credit may be granted, however, if the number of sales to a client is high or if the cost of a sale is significant. To minimize the loss of revenue resulting from accounts that cannot be collected, managers of sales and service outlets need to be aware of the Organization's credit and collection practices.

SCOPE

This policy applies to all general receivables.

POLICY

To establish guidelines for extending credit and thereby improve the Organization's cash flow.

EXTENDING CREDIT PRIVILEGES TO CLIENTS

1. The Chief Financial Officer will be responsible for establishing the credit limits that will be extended to individual clients. These limits must at all times protect the Organization's exposure to non-collectable accounts.

2. When goods or services in excess of ten thousand dollars ($10,000) are provided, and credit is being granted, a formal written agreement signed by two Directors[1] will be required.

3. Extension of credit beyond the standard thirty-day payment period[2] may only be granted when justified by unusual circumstances. In such situations, the extended credit terms must be shown on the face of the invoice and must have been agreed to by the Organization's Chief Financial Officer.

---

[1] Typically these members have been designated signing officers.
[2] The thirty-day period begins on the date that the invoice is prepared.

Criteria for Granting Credit

1. Granting credit is based on:

   - credit worthiness of the client
   - past payment record
   - amount of credit asked for

2. When a single sale is fifty dollars ($50) or less, only cash or check will be accepted as payment.

3. When a single sale is greater than fifty dollars ($50) the client may be invoiced. Credit terms of thirty days from date of the sale will apply and interest will normally be charged on overdue accounts.

4. The Goods and Service Tax *(if applicable to your state)* must be charged on all applicable sales. If the sale is tax exempt it must be indicated as such on the face of the invoice.

Collection of Accounts Receivable

1. Collection of general account receivables is the responsibility of the Chief Financial Officer. When a client contests the charge, the appropriate sales department will be responsible in resolving the contested items.

2. There will be a twenty-dollar ($20) service charge levied on all payments on account returned to the Organization by the payer's Bank.

Non-collectable Account and Write-offs

1. Clients who have failed to respond to collection notices will have their credit privileges withdrawn and a notice of cancellation of credit privileges will be forwarded to all sales departments. All future transactions with these clients will be on a cash only basis.

2. After all means of collection have been exhausted without success, the account receivable will be written-off and charged to the department that received the original credit. The Chief Financial Officer must approve all account write-offs.

3. Credit terms will not be granted other than through the practices stated by this policy.

FINANCIAL STATEMENTS AND RETURNS

Effective Date:
Cancels:
Dated:
Signature:
Position:

POLICY

Monthly financial statements will be available to the Board of Directors on demand. To provide an independent opinion of the Organization's financial well being an audit will be conducted annually. The Board of Directors will also ensure that returns and/or reports, such as the Annual Information Return, are submitted to the proper authority and within the allowed period of time.

PROCEDURE

1. Monthly financial statements will be provided to the Board of Directors, for review and approval, at each regular meeting of the Board of Directors. These statements will report the period's actual revenues and expenses, the year-to-date budget, a variance column reporting the difference between the two, and the approved annual budget. A written explanation will be required whenever the variance is deemed significant.[1]

2. The Office Administrator will prepare the annual financial statement for the Organization. Subsequent to the completion of the annual financial statement, and within 90 calendar days of the fiscal year-end, an independent audit will be completed. The audited statement will be prepared by a certified public accountant. The selection and the approval of the auditor will take place during the prior year's Annual General Meeting (AGM).

3. All receipts, statements, checks, Board minutes and other required information will be gathered together after year-end by the Office Administrator and made available to the auditor. A formal letter of engagement, which will include the start and the end date of the engagement, will be given to the auditor at this time.

4. A copy of the audited financial statements will be provided to all members of the Organization who attend the Annual General Meeting. The Treasurer, auditor or a designate will review the statements with the members present and a vote to accept the report will be held with the results of the vote recorded in the minutes of the meeting.

5. The Treasurer will present any recommendation made by the auditor to the Board of Directors at a regularly scheduled meeting of the Board of Directors. Recommendations will be discussed and adopted in principle by the Board of Directors if deemed appropriate.

6. An Annual Information Return must be completed and filed with the Internal Revenue Service no later than the fifteenth day of the fifth month following the Organization's fiscal year-end. The Office Administrator will complete and file this return within the allowable time.

---

[1] The term significant is subjective and each Board must determine the dollar amount that is appropriate for their Organization.

FLEXIBLE WORKING HOURS

Effective Date:
Cancels:
Dated:
Signature:
Position:

SCOPE

All full time permanent employees of the Organization.

POLICY

The flexible working hour system developed and adopted by the Organization allows all permanent full time employees to make responsible choices in adjusting their working hours according to the demands of their job and their own personal needs. Working within the flexible working hour system, permanent full time employees may arrive or leave their work position at anytime during any flexible time period.

Under the flexible working hour system each working day is divided into five periods, two core periods and three flex periods. Flex periods occur at the beginning and the end of each working day and at lunch. During any of these flex periods, employees are able to set their own work schedule according to the requirements of their work unit and their personal needs for time away from the job.

To be successful, a flexible work hour system requires the support of both management and employees. On occasion, supervisors must be willing to give of their own time to ensure adequate staffing. In general, work units where most of the employees work independent from one another, and where there is little personal interaction, are most likely to succeed with this system.

The Organization's flexible work hour system operates on a four week cycle. Work units are responsible for establishing their own core and flex periods. During a cycle an employee is required to work the standard number of hours plus or minus ten percent of that standard. By way of example, if there are twenty working days in a cycle and each day has the standard eight hours, then the allowable number of hours worked by an employee would range between a high of one-hundred seventy-six hours [160 hours x 110%] and a low of one-hundred forty-four hours [160 hours x 90%].

Credited hours may be consumed during flex periods or, with the prior approval of an employee's immediate supervisor during core periods. Any credit hours in excess of ten percent of the standard number of hours built up at the end of a cycle will be lost, unless special arrangements are made. In addition, an employee may not carry a deficit in work hours forward into the next cycle.

FUNDRAISING

Effective Date:
Cancels:
Dated:
Signature:
Position:

SCOPE

All fundraising activities conducted by the Organization.

POLICY

The Fundraising Committee is responsible for ensuring that the financial needs of the programs operated by fundraising dollars are met. The Fundraising Committee is also responsible for arranging, conducting and completing the activities outlined by the Annual Comprehensive Strategic Fundraising Plan and ensuring that all fundraising activities fall within the ethical guidelines established by the Organization.

The Fundraising Committee will meet no less than three times a year and will develop and monitor the Organization's Annual Comprehensive Strategic Fundraising Plan.

PROCEDURE

1. The fundraising needs and goals of the Organization will be determined each year by the Finance Committee and the Public Relations/ Fundraising sub-Committee.

2. All fundraising activities suggested for the Organization require the approval of the Board of Directors. Each year, on or before the due date for submission, the Executive Director will forward the Organization's Annual Comprehensive Strategic Fundraising Plan to the United Way (if applicable) for information.

3. At the minimum, an application for funding submitted by the Organization to the United Way must include the following:

   (a) a statement in which the Organization agrees to be governed by the United Way's Statement of Allocation Principles;
   (b) a completed Program and Financial Information form, and
   (c) any other supplementary information requested by the Community Services Committee of the United Way.

4. At a regularly scheduled meeting of the Board of Directors, the Executive Director will make available the annual review of the Agency Inclusion Agreement conducted by the Community Services Committee of the United Way.

5. The Executive Director, the Office Administrator or their delegate will secure and complete all the required licenses and permits for each fundraising event.

...Continued

6. The Executive Director, the Office Administrator or their delegate will determine what new accounts will be required to satisfy the security and fiduciary needs of each new fundraising activity and will also be responsible for reconciling and closing the accounts once the fundraising event has ended.

7. When applicable, the Office Administrator will mail tax receipts to all donors within five working days following the reconciliation of an event's revenue and expense accounts.

FUNDRAISING - SPECIAL INTEREST GROUPS

Effective Date:
Cancels:
Dated:
Signature:
Position:

PREAMBLE

In order to avoid possible conflicts while soliciting for funds during overlapping campaigns, guidelines must be established. The following guidelines will ensure that solicitations are properly coordinated by the Organization and that multiple visits to a single potential donor do not occur.

SCOPE

Any special interest group[1] or employee soliciting funds for, or on behalf of, the Organization.

POLICY

Any employee of the Organization, or any special interest group planning to solicit funds on behalf of the Organization, must first submit a written plan to the Organization's Fundraising Committee not less than ninety days in advance of the proposed event.

Each written plan will contain the following details:

1. Name of the special interest group
2. Name, address and telephone numbers of the organizers
3. The purpose of the fundraising project
4. The amount of funds the group hopes to raise from the solicitations
5. From what source(s) the special interest group intends to solicit funds
6. The proposed start date of the solicitation and its duration
7. Name of the contact person who will be responsible for the administration of the solicitation
8. Draft of solicitation material for approval, and
9. Name and account number that the special interest group wishes the funds to be directed to.

With the assistance of the Fundraising Committee, each special interest group or participating employee of the Organization must also compile and maintain the following records:

1. Lists of those to whom solicitations have been made
2. Lists of those who have donated gifts and the amount of the gift
3. Details on how funds expended, including amounts incurred in running the campaign.

The Organization's Fundraising Coordinator will ensure that each donor receives a letter of acknowledgement and a tax receipt, if appropriate.

---

[1] A special interest group is an organization that supports a specifically defined interest affiliated with the Organization.

FUNDRAISING - THE FUNDRAISING COMMITTEE

Effective Date:
Cancels:
Dated:
Signature:
Position:

POLICY

The Fundraising Committee will ensure that the fundraising goals of the Organization are met.

PROCEDURE

1. Prior to the end of the fiscal year the Executive Director and the Treasurer will meet with the chair of the Fundraising Committee to establish the Organization's fundraising goal for the upcoming year.

2. Within two months following the end of a fundraising event the Fundraising Committee will prepare a detailed report of the activity. The Executive Director, at a regularly scheduled meeting of the Board, will then table the report.

3. The Finance Committee will delegate persons to collect, count and deposit monies from each fundraising event. At the minimum, two delegates should be involved with each of these activities.

4. When appropriate, a sign out system will be used to control the distribution of fundraising tickets. Net funds and unused tickets from the activity will be reconciled during the event or immediately after the event ends.

5. The Fundraising Committee will ensure that all required federal, state and municipal licenses and/or permits are obtained in advance of the fundraising event.

6. All major fundraising projects planned for the Organization by the Fundraising Committee will be reviewed and approved by the Board of Directors and submitted to the United Way (if appropriate) for information.

7. A proper receipting system, acceptable to the Organization's external auditor, will be available to record the sale of merchandise sold directly by the Organization.

8. Tax receipts will be issued in accordance with the Organization's policy on tax receipting.

GARNISHEE OF WAGES

Effective Date:
Cancels:
Dated:
Signature:
Position:

POLICY

In compliance with federal and state law the Organization will accept all legal garnishments as ordered by the court. On receipt of a garnishment[1], the Organization will hold an employee's wages in trust, until a court order is received indicating satisfaction of the indebtedness or until ordered to surrender the monies to the court or its agent.

---

[1] A garnishment is a legal proceeding imposed by a court requiring payment of property to a third party to satisfy a creditor.

GIFTS PROVIDED BY THE ORGANIZATION

Effective Date:
Cancels:
Dated:
Signature:
Position:

SCOPE

All gifts to consumers, employees and volunteers of the Organization.

PURPOSE

To provide spending guidelines for purchasing gifts.

POLICY

Modest gifts may be purchased for staff and volunteers to recognize length of service, retirement or resignation from the Organization, or for some other special event or achievement. A gift or flowers may be provided for a birth, adoption, bereavement, marriage or any other significant event.

Modest gifts may also be purchased for consumers for a special occasion such hospitalization, bereavement, etc.

The cost of the gifts will follow common practice. In general length of service awards for employees will be kept within the following guidelines:

Between 5 and 10 years of service - gift not to exceed fifty dollars ($50)
Between 10 and 15 years of service - gift not to exceed one hundred dollars ($100)
Between 15 and 20 years of service - gift not to exceed one hundred and fifty dollars ($150), and
After 20 years of service - gift not to exceed two hundred dollars ($200).

HOSPITALITY EXPENSES

Effective Date:
Cancels:
Dated:
Signature:
Position:

PURPOSE

This policy establishes spending guidelines for hospitality expenditures. For the purpose of this policy, hospitality expenditures will include all costs that may be incurred by an employee while conducting the Organization's business with:

(a) on-site guests of the Organization
(b) off-site guests of the Organization
(c) employees of the Organization attending training or development sessions and,
(d) candidates on prearranged visits for employment interviews.

POLICY

This policy is designed to control costs and to expedite the reimbursement process for employees.

PROCEDURE

1. All approved hospitality expenditures will be coded to expense code 222[1] (Hospitality Expense) or to 244[1] (Interviewing Expense). The expense code that best represents the nature of the expense will be the code used.

2. Funds to offset hospitality expenditures will come from the department or program that has incurred the cost. It is therefore important for managers to consider this cost when developing their annual budget.

3. It may be possible to obtain additional funding for staff training or development when the Organization deems the cost necessary. In these situations, an application and cost submission should be forwarded to the Executive Director for consideration. Applications should be submitted not less than five working days before the event is scheduled to begin. If the application is approved, then the appropriate hospitality budget will be adjusted.

4. The department head will authorize and approve claims for reimbursement of personal expenditures made on behalf of the Organization. Claims in excess of one hundred dollars ($100) will require the signature of the Executive Director.

5. When large gatherings are planned, the expenditure may be billed directly to the Organization by completing a Purchase Requisition in advance of the event.

---

[1] Expense codes are used for illustration only.

INSURANCE - GENERAL COVERAGE

Effective Date:
Cancels:
Dated:
Signature:
Position:

POLICY

The Organization will provide insurance coverage that will fully protect its assets, employees, volunteers, visitors and its day to day business activities.

PROCEDURE

1. On an annual basis, the Executive Director will discuss the insurance requirements of the Organization with selected representatives from the insurance industry.

2. The Organization will ensure that its general liability insurance coverage is sufficient to adequately protect staff, volunteers, and visitors and all its assets.

3. At the minimum, the Organization's comprehensive insurance policy will include:

   (a) third party liability coverage
   (b) property insurance, including a tenant liability clause (if appropriate)
   (c) wrongful dismissal coverage
   (d) employee and Director's liability coverage and,
   (e) adequate coverage to recover losses resulting from errors of commission and/or omission.

4. To obtain the best value, insurance should be tendered every three years.

INSURANCE - RISK MANAGEMENT[1]

Effective Date:
Cancels:
Dated:
Signature:
Position:

POLICY

The Organization will provide insurance coverage that fully protects its assets, employees, volunteers and visitors, as well as its day to day business activities. To obtain the best insurance coverage, at the lowest possible price, the Organization will call for insurance tenders every three years.

On an annual basis the Executive Director will discuss the insurance requirements of the Organization with its carrier to ensure that its general liability insurance coverage is sufficient to adequately protect staff, volunteers and all of its assets. Furthermore, the Organization's comprehensive insurance[2] policy will also be reviewed and evaluated within the same time frame.

Any planned activity that is not normally part of the Organization's regular activities, and which has a risk component, must be reported to the Executive Director not less than ten working days prior to the commencement of the event. All accidents, property losses, injuries, and potential third party incidents must also be reported immediately to the Executive Director.

The Human Resources Department will be responsible for reducing the cost of personnel losses to both the individual and the Organization by providing employee claims administration, training, education and other types of personnel insurance coverage (benefits).

Under no circumstances may a department or an unauthorized individual initiate a claim or agree to a settlement or an action on behalf of the Organization.

---

[1] Risk management is the process of planning, organizing and controlling the resources and activities of the Organization in order to minimize the adverse effects of accidental losses. This includes the implementation of risk control practices, which promote the safety and well being of the Organization as a whole.

[2] Typically comprehensive coverage includes such things as third party liability, property insurance including a tenant liability clause (if appropriate), wrongful dismissal, and coverage to recover losses resulting from the commission of errors or omissions.

INTERNAL TRANSFER INVOICE

Effective Date:
Cancels:
Dated:
Signature:
Position:

SCOPE

All departments that transfer goods or services to or from other budget-funded areas within the Organization.

POLICY

This policy sets out the general guidelines for the Organization's charge-out and cost-recovery system. The inter-departmental transfer system has been implemented to control costs and to determine the actual dollar value of business conducted within the Organization itself. For the purpose of this policy, inter-departmental transfers will include products manufactured in one department and transferred to another department, external commodities purchased by one department and then transferred to other departments and the inter-departmental transfer of services. The cost of a transfer can be negotiated.

PROCEDURE

The Internal Transfer Invoice (ITI) consists of three pre-numbered sections. Each section is distinguishable by its unique color.

1. Either party involved in a transaction may originate the ITI.

2. The Internal Transfer Invoice is to be completed as follows:

Sold To:	*Enter name of buying or user department.*
Sold By:	*Enter name of selling department.*
Date:	*Enter the date of the sales transaction.*
Quantity:	*Enter number of units sold or hours of service provided.*
Description:	*Enter a brief description of the goods or service.*
Unit Price:	*Enter the unit price agreed on.*
Amount:	*Enter the total amount of the transaction.*

A separate line should be used for each type of good or service transferred.

The debit part of the transaction records the department receiving the good or service. The credit line reports the transferring or selling department. An ITI must be appropriately signed before it is posted to the Organization's ledgers.

3. Distribution

After the departments have agreed to the transaction, one of the parties begins the process of completing an ITI. The initiating party completes the appropriate section, signs it and then forwards it to the other party. Upon receipt the ITI is reviewed and if all looks to be in order, signed.

The third section (blue) of the completed form is then detached and filed. The remaining two sections are forwarded to the originating department. Once received, the originating department detaches the second section (yellow) for their records and sends the first section (white) to the accounting department for posting.

4. Control of Internal Transfer Invoice

To ensure that financial transactions conducted within the Organization are properly authorized and recorded it is imperative that Internal Transfer Invoices be controlled. This control is achieved when departments check to verify that the debits and credits on their month-end departmental expense statement are correct.

The ITI form is a multi-sectioned document requiring a number of processes to complete. To reduce costs, Internal Transfer Invoices should only be used when the value of the commodity or service being transferred exceeds fifty dollars ($50).

When multiple transactions of lesser amounts occur, it is recommended that costs be accumulated and then reported on a single ITI. It is important that costs do not straddle two fiscal years.

INTERNAL TRANSFER OF SERVICE DEPARTMENT COSTS

Effective Date:
Cancels:
Dated:
Signature:
Position:

SCOPE

All service departments[1] that have the authority to charge other departments within the Organization.

PURPOSE

To create an awareness of the costs involved in providing services internally and to help control the costs of internal service departments. This policy also provides guidelines that facilitate the internal distribution of services among departments and a consistent methodology of transferring those costs.

POLICY

For accounting purposes internally charged services are generally categorized into two types:

(a) Unit Requisitioned - when the price of the service is predetermined and where the user department exercises a large degree of control and,
(b) Central Service Standard - when the service provided is on going and not normally controlled by the user (costs may be influenced to some degree by the demand placed on the resource).

TRANSFER OF SERVICE COSTS

As defined above, the cost of Unit Requisitioned service is predetermined and the cost charged to the user department will normally be based on the actual cost to supply the service. If the requested service is expected to be long term then a standard monthly charge[2] or a single lump sum payment is acceptable.

Central Service Standards, such as the cost of operating the payroll and accounting departments, are not normally charged out to operating departments. Typically these types of costs are reported as indirect or overhead costs by the Organization. It is important, therefore, that central service costs be included when service departments establish their internal charge out rate, or when a department within the Organization charges externally.

Other Central Service Standards may include utilities, support services for grounds maintenance, janitorial and refuse removal, safety and fire protection, security and human resources.

---

[1] A Service Department is a department within the Organization whose primary purpose is to support a function within another department of the Organization.
[2] In most internal charge out systems the offsetting credit is posted to the department, or departments, providing the service.

...Continued

BUDGETING AND RECORDING

Service departments, other than Central Services, are funded by a budget allocation that is based on the estimated total gross operating expense of the department, less an estimated cost recovery amount.

Production-type departments, such as the central print shop, normally include all the actual costs of material, labor and departmental overhead when charging internally. Charges to clientele outside the Organization will normally have a percentage for profit added to them.

The budget allocation for Central Services[1] is normally established by examining actual costs from the prior fiscal year. Any relevant changes made to the Organization in the interim, however, should be taken into consideration when the new allocation amount is established.

[1] If a cost recovery system is established for Central Services then the charge out rate can be determined as above.

INVESTMENT AND BANKING GUIDELINES

Effective Date:
Cancels:
Dated:
Signature:
Position:

SCOPE

All banking and investment transactions entered into by the Organization.

POLICY

The Board of Directors is responsible for the security and preservation of the Organization's assets, capital, and reserves and will only accept investment risks common to its industry.

PROCEDURE

1. To optimize the Organization's financial position, the Executive Director and/or Treasurer will negotiate service charges and interest paid on deposits and investments with selected area banks and financial institutions. Such negotiations will be on going.

2. All excess cash will be invested at the direction of the Finance Committee. Investments will be limited to low, or no risk instruments, such as Guaranteed Investment Certificates or Government bonds or debentures. Investments will be limited to schedule "A" Banks or their equivalent. Investments in excess of two hundred and fifty thousand dollars ($250,000), and/or having a term greater than one year, will require the pre-approval of the Board of Directors.

3. At each Board meeting, the Treasurer will provide a detailed report on the status of each investment. At the minimum the report should include the type of investment held, the cost and the market value of the investment, the stated rate of return (if applicable), the maturity date and any re-investment alternatives.

INVESTMENT POLICY

Effective Date:
Cancels:
Dated:
Signature:
Position:

PREAMBLE

This policy identifies certain forms of investment that are intended to obtain a high degree of security and liquidity.[1] Whenever possible the maturity date of the investment should be arranged so as to coincide with specific or general operating cash requirements.

SCOPE

All short, medium and long-term investments made by, or on behalf of, the Organization.

OBJECTIVES

The security of the principal invested must be the first consideration in any investment and must be invulnerable by all reasonable credit tests. Although the need to maximize income is an important consideration, it should only be considered after the requirements of security and liquidity have been met.

POLICY

This policy is intended to provide limits within which the investment portfolio will operate. If a specific situation arises where it appears advantageous to go beyond these set limits then the prior written approval of the Board of Directors must be obtained. The performance of the investment portfolio will form part of the Treasurer's report and will be brought forward for information at each regular meeting of the Board of Directors.

It will be the Executive Director's and the Organization's Chief Financial Officer's responsibility to ensure that the investments in the portfolio are restricted to the following:

(a) Government - Any domestic or foreign government with a rating of not less than A1[2].
(b) Banks and other Financial Institutions - Any domestic or foreign Bank or Financial Institution with a rating of not less than AAA[2].

From time to time the Organization may deal in commercial paper or call loans. This policy does not include these investment alternatives.

---

[1] Liquidity is a measure of the time required to convert a security into cash with a minimum risk of capital loss. Liquidity is achieved by limiting the portfolio to readily marketable securities.

[2] As rated by Moody's Investors Service.

INVESTMENT POLICY

Effective Date:
Cancels:
Dated:
Signature:
Position:

SCOPE

All short, medium and long-term investments made by, or on behalf of, the Organization.

OBJECTIVES

The security of the principal invested must be the first consideration in any investment. Although the need to maximize income is an important consideration it should only be considered after the requirements of security and liquidity[1] have been met. To reaffirm this principle the Organization prefers that Schedule 1 banks hold its investments.

Whenever possible the maturity date of the investment should coincide with specific or general operating cash requirements.

POLICY

This policy is intended to provide limits within which the investment portfolio will operate.

To safeguard the capital of the investment portfolio a dollar limit of not less than seventy-five percent of the total value of the portfolio will be investment in financial instruments where the principal of the investment[2] is guaranteed. The Finance Committee, who will act on behalf of the Organization's Board of Directors, will establish the appropriate risk parameters for the balance of the invested funds.

If a specific situation arises where it appears advantageous to go beyond these set limits written approval of the Board of Directors must be obtained prior to the investment-taking place. It will be the Executive Director's and the Chief Financial Officer's responsibility to ensure that the investments in the portfolio are in agreement with this policy.

The performance of the investment portfolio will form part of the Treasurer's report and will be brought forward for information at each regular meeting of the Board of Directors.

---

[1] Liquidity is a measure of the time required to convert a security into cash with a minimum risk of capital loss. Liquidity is achieved by limiting the portfolio to readily marketable securities.

[2] Guaranteed Investment Certificate, Treasury Bills and Interest Bearing Notes are common examples of this type of secured investment.

MEMBERSHIP RECORDS

Effective Date:
Cancels:
Dated:
Signature:
Position:

SCOPE

All members of the Organization, past and present.

POLICY

A permanent record of all members, past and present will be maintained by the Organization. This record will include the member's name, telephone number and last known address. The record will also report details of any donations made by the member, the date that the donation was received and, if applicable, the amount receipted and the number of the tax receipt issued.

Such records will be maintained in a secure place and will be held in perpetuity.

OFFICERS AND SIGNING OFFICERS

Effective Date:
Cancels:
Dated:
Signature:
Position:

SCOPE

All contracts, documents or other instruments in writing that when signed legally bind the Organization to do, or not do, a defined thing.

PURPOSE

To identify the Officers of the Organization, and their respective responsibilities regarding the execution of documents, contracts and other instruments in writing.

DEFINITIONS

"Officer of the Board" will mean the Chair, Vice-Chair, Acting Chair, the Executive Director of the Organization, Chair of the Finance Committee, Chair of the Membership Committee, Secretary of the Board, and any other member the Board designates as an "Officer of the Board".

"Officer of the Organization" will mean the Executive Director, the Chief Financial Officer and any other employee that the Board designates as an "Officer of the Organization".

"Signing Officer" will mean any Officer of the Board and any Officer of the Organization so designated by the Board.

"Signing Authority" will mean any Officer of the Organization and any other person or persons so designated by the Board (e.g. Chair, Secretary, Chief Financial Officer, etc.).

POLICY

Any two Officers of the Board will sign all contracts, documents or other instruments in writing requiring execution by the Board, or on behalf of the Board. All such contracts, documents or other instruments in writing, so signed, will be binding on the Board without further authorization or formality.

All contracts, documents or other instruments in writing requiring execution by the Organization, or on behalf of the Organization, will be signed by any two Officers of the Organization, or by one Officer of the Board and by one Officer of the Organization. All such contracts, documents or other instruments in writing, so signed, will be binding on the Board and the Organization, without any further authorization or formality.

...Continued

SIGNING OFFICERS

The Board of Directors has duly appointed the following Signing Officers, for, and on behalf of, the Organization, effective *month, day, and year.*

Officers of the Board

- Chair of the Board *Name and Signature of Officer*
- Executive Director *Name and Signature of Officer*
- Chair of Finance Committee *Name and Signature of Officer*
- Chair of Membership Committee *Name and Signature of Officer*
- Secretary of the Board *Name and Signature of Officer*

Officers of the Organization

- Executive Director *Name and Signature of Officer*
- Chief Financial Officer *Name and Signature of Officer*
- Financial Officer *Name and Signature of Officer*

For ease of administration the Board may, from time to time, authorize certain employees of the Organization to execute contracts, documents and/or other instruments in writing.

ON-SITE ELECTION CAMPAIGNING

Effective Date:
Cancels:
Dated:
Signature:
Position:

POLICY

To establish guidelines for on-site[1]campaigning during municipal, state and federal elections. This policy does not limit any currently established policy that may be in effect.

PROCEDURE

Each candidate may arrange with the Executive Director the free use of a suitable meeting room for one on-site presentation to employees, volunteers, clients and visitors.

Each candidate, through the Executive Director, may make further bookings for the use of space. Those bookings will be subject to the appropriate fees as established by the Organization.

Candidates may arrange for one distribution of their campaign literature, through the Organization, by contacting the Executive Director not later than five working days before the literature is to be distributed. Candidates may arrange with the Executive Director, at that time, to place posters and bulletins on boards in designated areas.

---

[1] On-Site used within the text of this policy will mean all buildings and grounds that form part of the Organization's portfolio.

PAYROLL ADVANCES AND PAYROLL PURCHASE PLANS

Effective Date:
Cancels:
Dated:
Signature:
Position:

PREAMBLE

To assist employees in financial distress, the Organization may provide payroll advances. All such advances will be recovered within 30 calendar days from the date that the advance is issued. From time to time the Organization may also purchase a good or service on behalf of an employee through an employee purchase plan. Recoveries for such purchases will be through pre-approved payroll deduction.

SCOPE

All employees with the exception of the Executive Director (this limitation extends to payroll advance only).

PURPOSE

To establish guidelines for payroll advances and employee purchase plans.

POLICY

Payroll Advances

1. Employees may be granted one payroll advance in a single fiscal year unless otherwise approved by the Executive Director. Additional requests may be granted if they are related to a delay in receiving Workplace Safety and Insurance Board Benefits.

2. Payroll advances will not exceed the equivalent of two weeks gross pay for the employee based on their current guaranteed hours. For employees with no guaranteed hours, a payroll advance may not exceed the amount of vacation accrual available to the employee and any unpaid hours worked up to the date of the advance. Employees on a leave of absence are not eligible for a payroll advance.

3. The payroll advance must be repaid in full over the subsequent pay period, or in two equal payments over the following two pay periods. The Executive Director may grant an extension to the repayment period. This authorization must be in writing.

Employee Purchase Plans

1. The Finance/Administration Coordinator will establish the terms of each purchase plan agreement.

2. Factors that will be considered when approving participation in an employee purchase plan include the employee's guaranteed hours and his/her ability to meet the bi-weekly payroll deduction amount. Employees with no guaranteed hours might be able to participate as long as they have worked over

...Continued

fifteen (15) hours per pay period over the preceding three months and have confirmed their intent to work a sufficient number of hours to repay the debt.

PETTY CASH

Effective Date:
Cancels:
Dated:
Signature:
Position:

SCOPE

All Petty Cash Funds.

PURPOSE

From time to time the Organization is required to make cash purchases. This policy establishes the guidelines under which such purchases are to be conducted.

POLICY

To establish petty cash stations at a number of different locations within the Organization and to safeguard those stations by establishing and implementing appropriate guidelines.

PROCEDURE

1. A petty cash fund in the amount of two hundred and fifty dollars ($250) will be made available for the purchase of miscellaneous office materials and services.

2. Custody of the petty cash fund will reside with one employee.

3. Individual withdrawals from the fund will not exceed twenty-five dollars ($25) per voucher.

4. Expenditures from the fund must be accompanied by a proper receipt or voucher.

5. Receipts and vouchers will be kept with the petty cash fund.

6. The petty cash fund will be replenished when the balance in the fund falls below fifty dollars ($50).

7. The petty cash fund will be reconciled on a monthly basis by the Office Administrator in the presence of the custodian of the fund.

8. Periodically and without notice the petty cash fund will be reconciled by the Executive Director and/or Treasurer in the presence of both the Office Administrator and the custodian of the fund.

PETTY CASH IMPREST FUNDS

Effective Date:
Cancels:
Dated:
Signature:
Position:

SCOPE

All petty cash imprest funds.

POLICY

To establish petty cash stations within the Organization and to safeguard those stations by establishing and implementing proper controls.

PROCEDURE

Establishment Of Petty Cash Stations

The office administrator of the department requesting the petty cash station will make the request. The request will be in writing and will include:

(a) The name of the petty cash custodian.
(b) A plan for safekeeping the fund.
(c) The proposed level of the fund [special approval is required for stations that require more than five hundred dollars ($500)].
(d) The reason a petty cash station is required.

The Office Administrator of the department requesting the petty cash fund will assume the responsibility of regulating, delegating custodianship and ensuring the safekeeping of the fund. The Office Administrator may delegate the authority to approve petty cash disbursements to some other employee within the department. If a person other than the custodian is delegated to approve disbursements then a specimen signature of that person must be on file.

Disbursement From Petty Cash Funds

Individual petty cash purchases will not exceed seventy-five dollars ($75). Requests in excess of that amount will require a purchase requisition. Furthermore, petty cash funds will not be used to pay, in whole or in part, salaries or wages, personal loans or advances, or any purchase that benefits an employee, such as a personal gift.

Replenishment of Petty Cash

When a petty cash fund reaches the 50% level, or five working days before month-end, whichever occurs first, the petty cash custodian will apply to have the fund replenished.

THE PETTY CASH REPLENISHMENT ENVELOPE

When replenishment of the petty cash fund is required, the custodian will complete a petty cash replenishment envelope. The following sections of the replenishment envelope must be completed before the fund can be replenished:

(a) Sequential Number - The last number used on a replenishment envelope, plus one. All numbers must be accounted for and there must be no gaps in the sequence.
(b) Petty Cash Station Number - Insert the number of the petty cash station requesting the reimbursement.
(c) Department Number - Insert the department number having jurisdiction over the fund. If more than one department is using the station use separate envelopes for each department.
(d) Invoice, Date, Batch and Vendor Code - Leave blank. The accounting department will complete this section.
(e) Detail - In date sequence list each voucher paid and details as appropriate.
(f) Total - Insert the total of vouchers paid.
(g) Approved By - Obtain appropriate department signing authority.
(h) Cash Requested - In the block on the lower right-hand corner of the envelope insert the denominations of the cash required.
(i) Insert all original vouchers and receipts into the envelope and seal. Forward the envelope to the accounting department for audit and replenishment.

AUDIT OF VOUCHERS

1. The accounting department will audit the contents of petty cash envelopes by:

   (a) ensuring that the claim is supported by vouchers and/or receipts
   (b) ensuring that the coding section is complete and that all amounts are reported, and
   (c) ensuring erroneous vouchers, or vouchers that have not been coded or signed correctly are returned to the petty cash custodian for correction. In such instances the dollar amount of the rejected voucher will be deducted from the amount requested. All returned vouchers must be resubmitted after correction.

2. Upon completion of the audit, the vouchers and receipts will be returned to their envelope. The envelope will be marked **'VERIFIED'** and passed on to the Accounting Supervisor.

3. The Supervisor will add his or her name to the reimbursement envelope and then send it to the accounting clerk for reimbursement. Periodically, the Supervisor will remove the contents from the envelope to verify that the vouchers adequately support the amount of the claim.

4. After receiving the replenishment request, the accounting clerk will prepare the reimbursement and then notify the petty cash custodian. The custodian will then report to the accounting department where he/she will receive payment. The custodian will sign the 'Master Petty Cash Reimbursement Log' as proof of having received the funds.

The monthly departmental expenditure control report will reflect petty cash vouchers paid.

PHOTOCOPIER USAGE

Effective Date:
Cancels:
Dated:
Signature:
Position:

SCOPE

All employees of the Organization.

PURPOSE

To help manage the photocopying cost and to dissuade personal use of the Organization's photocopying equipment.

POLICY

Photocopy equipment and photocopy supplies are provided by the Organization to help its employee's better carry out their official duties. Personal usage, that is to say, usage other than that necessary to fulfill one's official duties, is strongly discouraged.

An employee, however, may be authorized to use the photocopy equipment and supplies for personal use, if permission is first granted by the employee's immediate supervisor.

If the number of personal use copies is small then the granting supervisor may wish to waive a usage fee. If the number of personal use copies is substantial, however, then a copy fee similar to that charged by local copy centers should be levied. Monies collected for personal use copies should be credited to the department responsible for managing the photocopying budget. All authorized personal use copying should be conducted outside the regular business hours of the Organization.

PROGRAM OR PROJECT CANCELLATION

Effective Date:
Cancels:
Dated:
Signature:
Position:

SCOPE

All externally restricted donations accepted by the Organization where the object for the contribution is subsequently cancelled.

POLICY

It is the responsibility of the Organization to contact all donors who have contributed to a specific program or project when that program or project is cancelled and significant funds remain unspent.

PROCEDURE

1. In the event that a program or project is cancelled, the Executive Director will contact all donors who have made a contribution to that program or project within thirty calendar days of its cancellation. The Executive Director will then ask permission to redirect their contribution. If the donor gives permission to redirect the contribution a letter of appreciation, signed by the Executive Director, will be issued within five working days.

2. If permission to redirect a special purpose contribution is not given by the donor then all or part of the contribution will be returned to the donor with a letter of acknowledgement. In such cases the Organization must ensure that any tax receipt issued as the result of the original contribution is returned and made void.

REBATES AND TAX EXEMPTIONS

Effective Date:
Cancels:
Dated:
Signature:
Position:

SCOPE

All tax rebates, tax exemptions and product rebates.

POLICY

1. All material tax rebates and other credits will be applied for on a timely basis with the credit allocated to the respective budget and/or department that gave rise to the expenditure.

2. All tax exemptions available to the Organization will be used to offset taxes payable.

3. The Organization will be identified as the payee on all rebate applications for goods and/or services purchased by the Organization.

PROCEDURE

The Finance/Administrative Coordinator will prepare all rebate applications and ensure that a designated signing authority signs them.

Documentation detailing how the rebate is calculated will be kept, at least until the rebate is received. An account receivable will be established for each rebate applied for. Any discrepancies between the account receivable and the actual rebate received will be investigated.

If an external consultant is contracted to prepare the rebate application, a fee will be established before proceeding with the application. The consultant will receive payment only after the rebate is received. Where the amount to be paid is based on a percentage of the rebate receivable any adjustment to that amount will be reflected in the amount paid to the consultant.

REIMBURSEMENT OF HOSPITALITY EXPENSE

Effective Date:
Cancels:
Dated:
Signature:
Position

SCOPE

All staff.

POLICY

To establish a process that will reimburse personnel and pay suppliers for eligible Hospitality expenses.

PROCEDURE

Hospitality expenses incurred by personnel may be claimed as follows:

1. By completing and submitting a Travel Authority and Expense report as required for travel expenditure claims. Claims for personal reimbursement should indicate the number of guests and the reason for the expense. Supporting documents, such as a receipt for a meal or a parking permit, should be attached to the claim whenever possible.

2. By Purchase Order for prearranged larger group luncheons or activities. The Purchase Order will serve as the authorization from the Organization to allow a supplier to invoice costs directly to the Organization. To initiate a Purchase Order, an authorized purchase requisition is required. When completing the purchase requisition the following information will be required:

   (a) the name of the group and the number of guests in the party
   (b) where the event is to take place, if different from the supplier's address
   (c) date and time of the event and,
   (d) the prearranged cost to be invoiced to the Organization.

   The purchase requisition will be forwarded to the purchasing department where it will be assigned a Purchase Order number and then sent to the supplier.

SHARED POSITION

Effective Date:
Cancels:
Dated:
Signature:
Position:

SCOPE

All permanent full time employees.

PURPOSE

To improve the Organization's working environment.

POLICY

The Organization recognizes that employees may wish to share their employment position. Furthermore, the Organization will assist in setting up shared positions, if it can be demonstrated that the duties of the position can be discharged effectively under a shared position arrangement, and suitably qualified candidates for sharing the position, can be found.

PROCEDURE

1. The employee, as the primary incumbent wishing to share their position, is responsible for completing the Position Share Application. (PSA).

2. Once the PSA is completed, it will be reviewed by the primary incumbent's immediate supervisor. At this time, potential candidates for the position share will be discussed. It is the responsibility of the primary incumbent to locate a suitably qualified candidate, the secondary incumbent.

3. Details regarding the number of hours worked, days worked, and duties to be performed, will be developed by the two incumbents. These arrangements must also meet the approval of the immediate supervisor.

4. There is no time limit on a position share. There will however, be a six month trial period. During this period, the arrangement may be terminated with a two week written notice by either of the two incumbents or by the supervisor. If, after the trial period, the supervisor believes that the position share is not working to the betterment of the department, he/she may ask that the arrangement be dissolved. If the incumbents do not agree with their supervisor's assessment, then the incumbents may appeal that decision to senior management.

5. After the six month trial period the primary incumbent may, with one months notice to his/her supervisor and the secondary incumbent, terminate the position share agreement.

6. If the primary incumbent leaves the shared position, for any reason, then that shared position will return to its original full time status. At that time the position will be declared vacant and it will be posted.

SITE LICENSE

Effective Date:
Cancels:
Dated:
Signature:
Position:

SCOPE

The Organization will obtain site licenses for software products based primarily on economic viability and concurrence with the Computing Department's list of supported products.

POLICY

A site license grants the Organization certain rights to copy and distribute software within its jurisdiction. A site license does not include other forms of licenses such as single copy licenses or bulk order licenses. Negotiations and processing for these types of licenses are the responsibility of the Purchasing Department.

PROCEDURE

1. Acquisition of Software

   Proposals for the acquisition of site licenses should be forwarded to the Director of the Computing Department. Each proposal should include the following:

   (a) Product name and description
   (b) Availability of site license
   (c) Terms and conditions associated with acquisition
   (d) Cost of acquisition
   (e) Evidence of departments and users who are interested in acquiring the software.

2. Process of Approval and Product Distribution

   (a) The Director of the Computer Department will examine all proposals received and will determine the advisability of entering into each site license agreement. Decisions will be based on potential economic benefits. Should there be any questions or concerns about the Organization's ability to meet the terms and conditions of the agreements, the Director of the Computer Department will refer the matter to the Organization's solicitors for advice.
   (b) All negotiations, including prices, and terms and conditions, will be the responsibility of the Purchasing Department.
   (c) Based on the number of copies purchased and the cost of acquiring and administering the site license agreements, the Director of the Computer Department will determine the price that will be charged to internal users (this assumes that the Organization operates an internal cost recovery system).
   (d) After the execution of the necessary documents to meet the terms and conditions of the site license agreement, the Purchasing Department will distribute the product.

3. Responsibilities

(a) The Computing Department will be responsible for the administration of site licenses. It will also communicate with users regarding the availability of various microcomputer software products and with other like organizations regarding joint site licensing.
(b) The Computing Department will maintain a database of software products available to the Organization. It will also be responsible for publishing acquisition information to the broader community within the Organization.
(c) The Purchasing Department will advise the Computing Department of any volume discount pricing arrangements negotiated on behalf of the Organization.

SOFTWARE PURCHASES AND SITE LICENSING

Effective Date:
Cancels:
Dated:
Signature:
Position:

SCOPE

All software products and site licensing[1] agreements in excess of one thousand dollars ($1,000). The terms "software product" and "site-license" may be used interchangeably in this policy.

POLICY

Prior to purchasing software or entering into a site-licensing agreement, the Organization will thoroughly research the product for price, compatibility and effectiveness. The Organization will also do everything reasonable to ensure that the product, once purchased, is adequately safeguarded and used strictly as intended.

PROCEDURE

1. The Finance/Administration Coordinator will determine if the Software Company offers any Charitable Giving Programs to non-profit Organizations. If such programs exist the Coordinator will then prepare a written request to the vendor asking that the product be provided free of charge or at a reduced cost.

2. Prior to purchasing any software product, the Finance/Administration Coordinator will prepare a formal proposal that will be reviewed by the Executive Director. At the minimum the proposal will include an explanation as to why the product is needed, the name of the product, the preferred vendor and the cost. To ensure that the Organization obtains the best possible price no less than two additional quotes must be obtained from creditable vendors.

3. The Executive Director must approve all software purchases that fall within the scope of this policy.

4. All original software must be forwarded to the Finance/Administration Coordinator for safekeeping.

5. All software purchased by the Organization is for its sole and exclusive benefit. Copies will not be provided to staff, consumers, volunteers or other Organizations.

---

[1] A site license grants the owner, or in some cases the lessee, the right to copy and distribute a specific software product within its own jurisdiction.

TAX RECEIPTED DONATIONS

Effective Date:
Cancels:
Dated:
Signature:
Position:

SCOPE

All significant donations where the donor is known.

POLICY

1. The Organization will receipt and acknowledge all significant gifts received from known donors.

2. Official tax receipts will be issued and maintained in accordance with the regulations set out by the Internal Revenue Service.

PROCEDURE

1. A permanent record of all gifts donated to, and accepted by, the Organization will be maintained. At the minimum each record will include the date the gift was accepted, the full name and address of the donor, the nature of the donation and the number of the tax receipt issued.

2. Tax receipts will be issued within five working days from the date that the gift is accepted.

3. The signature of the Executive Director or designate is required on all tax receipts.

4. Blank tax receipts will be kept on site in a secure place. Access will be restricted to the Finance/Administration Coordinator, the Executive Director and their designate.

5. All tax receipts must be accounted for and maintained in numerical sequence. Spoiled tax receipts will be retained and marked void. All receipts will be retained for a minimum of seven calendar years from the date of issue. A written report will be required whenever a tax receipt is missing. The report will include the number of the missing tax receipt, the date that the loss occurred or was discovered, and an explanation of the loss. The report will be signed by the Finance/Administration Coordinator, the Executive Director and by any other employee of the Organization whose name appears in the report.

6. Tax receipts will not be backdated.

7. An Annual Information Return will be completed and filed with the Internal Revenue Service within the required timeframe.

8. As is required by Generally Accepted Accounting Principles (GAAP) donated goods are to be recorded as revenue in the fiscal year that they are accepted.

TELEPHONE USAGE

Effective Date:
Cancels:
Dated:
Signature:
Position:

SCOPE

All employees of the Organization.

PURPOSE

To manage the cost of long distance telephone charges and to help ensure that telephone lines are available to conduct the Organization's business.

POLICY

Telephones are only to be used to conduct the Organization's business. Under certain circumstance, however, employees may be authorized to make personal calls. In general, personal calls may be made when:

1. The calls do not adversely affect the Organization or the employee's ability to carryout his/her official duties.

2. The calls are of a reasonable duration and frequency.

3. The calls cannot be reasonably made outside of business hours.

In addition to the above, a personal call will be authorized when:

1. An employee is required to work overtime without advance notice and the call is to advise his/her family of the change in schedule, or to make alternative transportation or care arrangements for a dependent.

2. An employee makes a brief call to speak to a spouse, a child, an elderly parent, or someone responsible for them, such as a school, day care center or a nursing home.

3. An employee calls a person or an Organization, such as a physician or a government office, which can only be reached during business hours.

4. An employee makes a brief call to arrange for emergency repairs to his/her residence or vehicle.

5. While on official business an employee makes a call, of five minutes or less, to announce their safe arrival, delay, or change of plan.

The Organization is not responsible for any costs for calls made under the terms of this policy. All calls must be either local, made to an 800, 888 or some other toll-free number, or must be charged to the home telephone number of the employee making the call.

RESPONSIBILITIES AND APPEALS

The department head for each unit is responsible for monitoring any use of the Organization's telephones beyond the limitations of this policy. Department heads are also responsible for collecting telephone costs that have been charged to the Organization and are the result of a chargeable, non-authorized personal call made by an employee. All such monies collected will be delivered to the accounting department where it will be properly coded to the appropriate account and receipted. The second copy of the receipt will be given to the payer as proof of payment.

Departments may choose to implement their own telephone policies that further restrict the use of departmental telephones, such policies however should not be seen as replacing or modifying the Organization's policy on telephones.

If disciplinary action is taken based on alleged violation of the Organization's Telephone Usage Policy, the employee may pursue whichever action is available to them, in their collective bargaining agreement.

TRAVEL

Effective Date:
Cancels:
Dated:
Signature:
Position:

SCOPE

All employees of the Organization who travel on authorized business.

PURPOSE

To acknowledge the need for employees to travel while conducting the Organization's business and to provide guidelines for the reimbursement of approved expenses incurred during those trips.

POLICY

The Organization will reimburse employees for reasonable and justifiable out-of-pocket expenses incurred while traveling on behalf of the Organization.

The Organization will also reimburse the expenses incurred by employees required to work off-site on a temporary basis. Employees hired to work off-site on a full-time basis, however, will not normally be reimbursed for their expenses unless otherwise directed by the Executive Director.

In the event that a cash advance is needed for an authorized business trip, or where the anticipated cost of the trip is expected to exceed two thousand dollars ($2,000), an approved "Travel Authority Claim" will be required. When abnormal or unusual expenses are incurred on behalf of the Organization while traveling, a detailed written explanation of those expenses must be provided to the proper authority for validation of the claim. Travel Authority Claims should be submitted no later than ten working days after the completion of the trip.

AUTHORIZATION AND APPROVAL

A Signing Officer may delegate signing authority for reimbursements of less than five hundred dollars ($500). This delegation of authority must be approved by the Executive Director and must be in writing. Delegation does not dilute the overall responsibility of the original Signing Officer. A specimen signature of the delegate must be forwarded to the Chief Financial Officer.

TRAVEL ADVANCES

An outstanding travel advance must be settled before a new advance can be requested. Arrangements may be made for a standing travel advance where circumstances warrant. Application for standing advances should be made to the Chief Financial Officer by the employee's supervisor.

...Continued

TRANSPORTATION

When reviewing Travel Authority Claims, the authority or delegate should ensure that the most economical travel option has been selected. When a private automobile is used, for example, the claim for reimbursement cannot exceed the cost of normal public transportation. Public transportation can be arranged through local travel agents and invoiced directly to the Organization.

Air travel may be utilized when the cost compares favorably with other modes of transport or when the urgency of the commitment makes it necessary. In such circumstances, employees will be limited to the economy fare. First class fare will be allowed only if economy fare is unavailable. Air travel can be arranged through local travel agents and invoiced directly to the Organization.

Travel to and from the airport is available through many local transport service companies. If a private automobile is used, then the Organization's mileage allowance will be in effect to calculate the reimbursement. Reasonable and supported parking charges may also be reimbursed. The total round trip cost claimed, for the use of a private vehicle, cannot exceed the total round trip cost of the most economical local limousine service.

Air insurance will be allowed up to a maximum of one hundred thousand dollars ($100,000) of coverage. This cost needs to be supported by a receipt or the insurance policy. Many travel agencies will provide this coverage free of charge.

ACCOMMODATION

Hotel, motel and other accommodation expenses will be reimbursed if properly supported. Supporting documents should report the location of the stay, the dates, and the daily or weekly rate.

When an employee shares a room with a family member who is not an employee of the Organization, then only the single person charge should be claimed.

Accommodation provided in private residences may be reimbursed at the discretion of the employee's approving authority. Under no circumstances, however, should this amount exceed the rates authorized by the Organization.

MEALS

Actual out-of-pocket meal costs incurred while traveling on the Organization's business will normally be reimbursed without receipts. Whenever exceptionally large amounts are claimed for individual meals however, a written explanation to the appropriate signing authority will be required. The current daily meal allowance of forty-five dollars ($45) may be used as a guideline.

Tips are also considered to be an allowable expense. No receipts are required for Tips but they must be reasonable.

...Continued

Telephone and Fax Messages

To reduce administrative paper work, employees communicating with the Organization are requested to send messages collect, or have the charges reversed whenever possible. Claims for reimbursement will only be honored when such costs are incurred on behalf of the Organization.[1]

Taxicabs

Supported claims for taxi fares are allowable but may be reduced if considered unnecessary or excessive.

Hospitality to Guests

When traveling, expenses may be claimed for hospitality to guests. Such costs, however, must be reasonable and must not exceed the Organization's Policy on Hospitality.

Traffic Summonses and Other Penalties

Expenses incurred in the payment of fines, include parking fines and other such penalties, will be disallowed.

Other unspecified expenses incurred on behalf of the Organization while traveling may be reimbursed if appropriately supported. In general, approved Travel Authority Claims of less than seventy-five dollars ($75) will be satisfied through petty cash.

[1] Reasonable communication costs to an employee's home may be reimbursed at the discretion of the approving authority.

TRAVEL AND OTHER ELIGIBLE COSTS

Effective Date:
Cancels:
Dated:
Signature:
Position:

POLICY

To provide employees with spending guidelines while conducting the Organization's business.

PROCEDURE

Conference, workshop and travel expenses incurred by an employee while performing his/her duties will be reimbursed subject to the prior approval of the Executive Director. The Board President will approve such expenditures when incurred by the Executive Director.

Reimbursements must be within the amounts established by the Board and may include:

(a) mileage or public transportation costs
(b) airline and taxi fares
(c) cost of breakfast, lunch, and dinner (dollar limits in effect)
(d) reasonable incidental costs incurred during the business outing and,
(e) overnight accommodations.

The comparative lowest cost will be balanced against efficiency and reasonableness.

1. The Executive Director will authorize the reimbursement of registration and travel costs incurred by a volunteer while performing his/her duties at the request of the Organization. In such situations the volunteer must obtain written approval from the Executive Director before the expense is incurred.

2. The Human Resources Committee will review all allowances and dollar limits annually and will recommend revisions to the Board of Directors, as necessary.

3. An official pre-printed Travel claim must be submitted within three months of the first occurrence. The claim should include the nature of the business and the distance traveled. Each claim should be dated and signed by the person submitting it. The signature of the Executive Director on the claim will act as the authority for reimbursement.

TELEPHONE AND FAX

Long distance telephone calls and faxes should be limited to business only. If chargeable personal calls need to be made then they should be charged to the individual's home phone number. The Office Administrator will review all telephone bills for compliance.

TRUST AND SPECIFIC PURPOSE FUNDS

Effective Date:
Cancels:
Dated:
Signature:
Position:

GENERAL

The Organization is the recipient of a wide variety of trust and specific purpose, or restricted funds. These funds may include gifts, grants, awards, or contracts and agreements with individuals, businesses, corporations and foundations. Funds are commonly received in the form of cash, check or donations in kind. Funds can be endowed, where only the interest earned on the donation is expendable, or the donation can be totally expendable. The degree of restriction is dependent on the donor. In general, trust and specific purpose funds are donated for specific purposes by documents such as a deed of trust or will. Typically these funds are administered, accounted for, and reported individually so that the intended purposes and terms of the donation are met.

The Board of Directors of the Organization may also establish trust and specific purpose funds. These funds may be created from the general revenues of the Organization or from non-restricted donations. These types of funds are sometimes referred to as quasi-endowment funds because the Board of Directors may change the purposes and terms of these endowed funds at will.

The Board of Directors may also choose to set aside special expendable funds for management purposes. These funds are often referred to as Designated Funds and may include special funds to other groups or individuals.

INFORMATION REQUIREMENTS

To properly discharge the obligations of a trust, specific purpose or restricted fund, the Organization will document the following information for each fund:

The detailed purpose of the donation, or revenue, used to create the fund.

1. The purpose and terms of the fund.

2. If the donation used to create the fund was not in the form of cash or a cash equivalent, then the market or assessed value of the donation must be reported, along with an accurate description of the asset received.

3. If the fund is expendable or endowed. If endowed then the disposition of interest earned on the donation must be detailed.

4. The address of the client or sponsor as well as the address of the office to which reports or any other acknowledgement should be sent as per the terms of accepting the donation.

5. The starting date of the agreement, the period, and the termination date if specified.

6. The disposition of any remaining balance in the fund at the end of a specified term must also be stipulated. This information will assure that the fund is appropriately closed and cleared into the accounts of the donor, the sponsor and/or the Organization.

Any other instruction that would promote the efficient administration of a fund should also be included.

As the paying agent, the Organization is responsible to collect and remit income tax, federal and/or state pension payments, employment insurance and other statutory benefits.

ACCOUNTABILITY

Trust and special purpose funds are recorded and maintained in a separate ledger by the Organization's accounting office.

The accounting office is responsible for:

1. Assigning a unique identifying number for each trust or special purpose fund. These unique numbers help associate the fund with the terms and conditions of the deed of trust, will, or other document of agreement under which the fund was created. This association will help ensure that the terms of the agreement are followed.

2. Establishing the ledgers and the methods necessary to accurately and effectively record and report the financial activities of the fund to donors, sponsors and the Organization's Board of Directors.

3. Ensuring the financial reports are in the manner described within the terms of the deed of trust, will, or other document of agreement.

4. Maintaining files and records in sufficient detail so as to make them suitable for internal, external and corporate or government audit.

5. Ensuring that invoices and other claims are paid by the fund within appropriate time limits and that the accounts receivable due to the fund are collected and credited appropriately.

6. Corresponding with appropriate agencies and clients of the Organization to discharge the above mentioned responsibilities.

SAFEGUARDS AND CONTROL

Managing restricted funds requires a high level of control. This needs to be considered when funding agreements are being negotiated with donors and sponsors. The accounting office has developed the following reports and routines that will help safeguard the assets of the Organization's restricted funds and ensure that minimum audit requirements are met, or exceeded.

REPORTS AND STANDARD STATEMENTS

1. Expenditures and revenues by line item and source.
2. Current expenditure and revenue totals.
3. Month-end expenditure and revenue totals.
4. Fiscal year-end expenditure and revenue totals.
5. Year over year comparative (five year minimum).
6. Opening fund balance for start of new fund year.
7. Budget allotment (if applicable).
8. Current unexpended fund balance.

If a trust or special purpose fund is over spent at the end of a fiscal year, the department responsible for managing the fund may be required to make up the difference from their own department.

UNBUDGETED EXPENSES

Effective Date:
Cancels:
Dated:
Signature:
Position:

SCOPE

Unbudgeted expenditures, and purchase commitments that extend over two fiscal year-ends and exceed two thousand dollars ($2,000).

POLICY

The Board of Directors must approve payments for any unbudgeted item that exceeds two thousand dollars ($2,000). To ensure that the best possible price has been secured for the Organization, a minimum of three written quotes is required for such purchases. If the expenditure is the result of an emergency, then the consent of any two of the following three persons will be sufficient, the Executive Director, the President and/or the Treasurer.

Details of all emergency purchases will be discussed at the next regularly scheduled meeting of the Board of Directors.

WAIVER OF NON-EMPLOYEE ON SITE LIABILITY REQUIREMENT

Effective Date:
Cancels:
Dated:
Signature:
Position:

PREAMBLE

This policy is intended to acquaint persons with the inherent risks involved while working on the Organization's property and to notify them that they are not covered by Worker's Compensation. The policy also wishes to ensure that persons agree to save harmless the Organization should an occurrence arise on site, which causes that person damage or loss.

SCOPE

All non-employees invited by the Organization to work on site, without charge, must complete a Waiver of Liability Form.

POLICY

All employees of the Organization authorized to invite, arrange and/or approve of non-employees working on site, without-pay, must assure that a Waiver of Liability form has been signed by that person prior to beginning the work, and that a completed copy has been provided to the Organization's personnel office.

Waivers will be dated for a period of no longer than 12 consecutive months, starting from the date that the work begins. A sample "Waiver of Liability" follows.

WAIVER OF LIABILITY

NAME OF VISITOR:
ADDRESS:
TELEPHONE NUMBER:

I, ______________________________ hereby release and forever discharge the Organization, and members of the Organization, from all claim demands, damage actions or causes of action arising from my work while on the Organization's premises. I further release the Organization and its servants from all claims or demands whatsoever in law or in equity.

This waiver is to remain in force for a period of one year from the date of signing or the duration of the working period whichever is less.

WHEREOF I have signed as having read and understood the content,

This _______________ day of _________ 20__.

Authority's Signature _______________ Person's Signature _______________.

Section II

NOTES TO THE FINANCIAL STATEMENTS

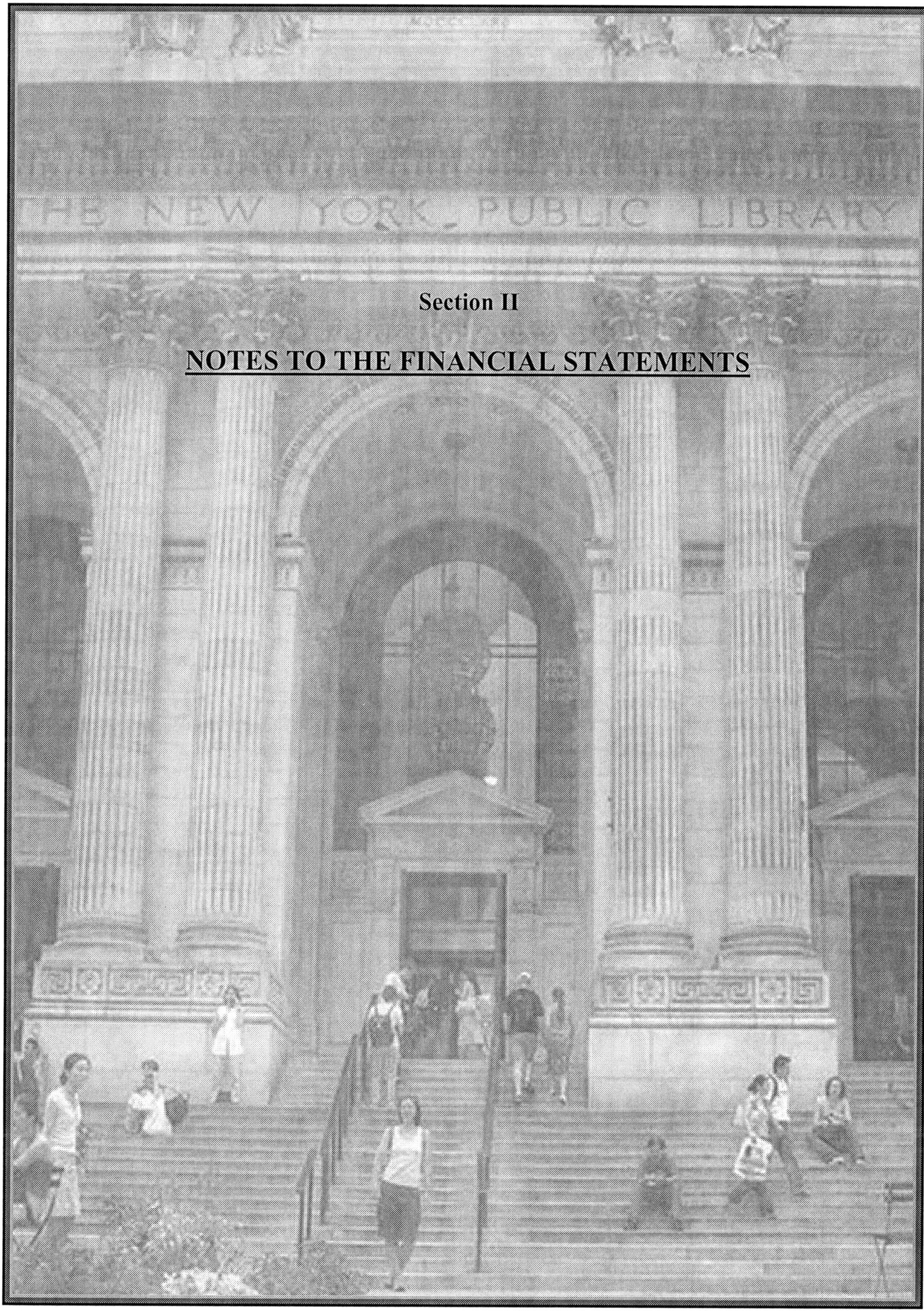

INTRODUCTION TO NOTES TO THE FINANCIAL STATEMENTS

This section is divided into two parts. The first part includes a number of sample notes that would be found in the year-end audit reports of most not-for-profit Organizations. The second part contains a full set of notes for a medium to large sized Organization that we have simply called - **THE ORGANIZATION**.

Notes accompany financial statements to help readers better understand the numbers being reported. As many Directors of small Organizations do not have the skills required to properly read and understand the financial data provided to them it is particularly important that they be given a good set of notes. The same can also be said of general members, who often are responsible for approving the Organization's year-end audited report at the AGM (annual general meetings).

The sample notes that follow are not inclusive. There may be times when you require a note and no sample is provided. These occasions, however, should be rare.

To satisfy personal preference more than one sample note has been provided for a number of subjects.

Helpful Hints:

- Your year-end audit report should include as many notes as it takes for your readers to understand the financial data reported.
- Each year the Finance Committee should review the notes.
- If a note no longer applies - exclude it.
- If currently there is no note, but there should be - write one.
- The best note is simple, short and clear.
- For clarity, consider including a table with your note.
- Notes should reflect the practices and policies of the Organization.
- Better questions will be asked at your AGM if good notes are part of your year-end audited report.

TABLE OF CONTENTS

SAMPLE NOTES
TO FINANCIAL STATEMENTS

Accrual Accounting

The Organization follows the accrual basis of accounting by recording income when earned and expenses when materials or services are received. Commitments for goods and services not yet received are not included in expenses.

Pledges from fundraising and other donations, because of the uncertainty of receipt, are not recorded until the donations are actually received.

Ancillary Enterprises

Charges are made to ancillary enterprises for all costs associated with these operations, including replacements and renovations of equipment and facilities. The enterprises are self-sustaining and are intended to operate on a breakeven basis. Any profit or loss from ancillary operations are added to, or deducted from, the reserve of the enterprise.

Appropriations of Fund Balances

The Organization appropriates a portion of its Operating Net Assets for specific future uses. When incurred, related expenses are charged to operations and the balance of the appropriation is reduced accordingly.

Appropriations of Fund Balances

Appropriations are restrictions of fund balances designated for:

(a) future purchase order commitments,
(b) capital and renovation projects committed but not yet completed,
(c) unspent Organizational unit funds permitted to be carried forward at the end of each fiscal year for expenditure in the following year and,
(d) contingencies in such amounts as are deemed necessary by the Board of Directors.

Benefit Program

Under agreements with various employee groups the Organization is committed to provide certain benefits to both active and retired employees. These benefits include life insurance, long-term disability and major medical and dental coverage. It is the Organization's policy to record the premiums paid to fund these plans as an expense in the year incurred. To partially offset estimated liabilities of the program, any reserves arising from these plans are held by the benefit program administrator.

Building Campaign

In order to fund a major expansion to the Organization's building, a capital building campaign was launched to raise $750,000 by the year 20xx. The $100,000 of deferred building campaign contributions reported is comprised of $90,000 contributed to date and externally restricted investment income of $10,000.

Capital Assets

Purchased capital assets are recorded at cost. Contributed capital assets are recorded at fair market value at the date of contribution, except for land received under the terms of a grant, which is carried at nominal value. Capital assets are amortized on a straight-line basis over their estimated useful lives.

Contributions received for capital assets are deferred in the accounts and amortized over the same time period and on the same basis as the capital assets they relate to.

Capital Assets
Purchased capital assets are recorded at cost. Contributed capital assets are recorded at fair value at the date of contribution. Amortization is provided on a straight-line basis over the assets' estimated useful life, which for buildings is 40 years and for equipment 10 years.

Capital Assets
Purchased capital assets are recorded at cost. Contributed capital assets are recorded at fair market value at the date of contribution. Capital assets are amortized on a straight-line basis over their estimated useful lives:

Buildings	40 years
Parking lots and roadways	15 years
Furniture and equipment	10 years
Computer equipment	3 years
Vehicles	5 years

Contributions received for capital assets are deferred in the accounts and amortized over the same term and on the same basis as the related capital assets.

Capital Leases
The Organization has entered into certain leases for which title to the related assets will vest in the Organization on termination of these leases. The original cost of the assets is reflected in capital assets. In addition, the present value of the outstanding lease commitments is reflected as an obligation under capital leases.

Cash and Cash Equivalents
Cash and cash equivalents include all highly liquid interest-bearing deposits and short-term investments with maturity dates of three months or less at time of purchase.

Commitments
Costs to complete major capital projects in progress as at March 31, 20xx are estimated to be $3,500,000 *(include prior year comparative)* and will be funded by government grants, gifts and the resources of the Organization.

Comparative Figures
Some of the prior year's comparative figures have been reclassified to conform to the current year's presentation.

Comparative Figures
Some of the prior year's comparative figures have been reclassified to conform to the financial statement presentation adopted in the current year.

Contingent Liabilities
The Organization has been named as a defendant or co-defendant in several actions for damages. The outcome and the amount of the losses, if any, are not determinable at this time and accordingly, no provision for losses has been made in the financial statements. The amount will be accounted for in the period when, and if, such losses are determined.

Contingent Liabilities
The Organization is the defendant of several unresolved statements of claims. It is not expected that the ultimate outcome of these claims will have a material effect on the financial position of the Organization.

Contributed Services
The Organization acknowledges the receipt of donated services. However, because of the difficulty of determining their fair market value, donated services are not recognized in the financial statements.

Contributed Services
Volunteers contribute approximately 400 hours to assist the Organization in carrying out its services. However, because of the difficulty of determining their fair value, contributed services are not recognized in the financial statements.

Contributed Services
Volunteers contribute an indeterminable number of hours per year to assist the Organization in carrying out its services. Due to the difficulty of determining their fair value, contributed services are not recognized in the financial statements.

Contributed Services
Due to the difficulty of determining their fair market value, contributed services are not recognized in the financial statements.

Deferred Contributions and Deferred Capital Contributions
Deferred contributions represent unspent externally restricted grants, donations and investment income.

Deferred capital contributions represent the unamortized amount of grants, donations and investment income received for the purchase of capital assets. The amortization of deferred capital contributions is recorded as income in the statement of operations.

Deferred Contributions and Deferred Capital Contributions
Deferred contributions represent unexpended amounts, which are subject to externally imposed restrictions. Deferred capital contributions represent the unamortized amount of grants and donations used for the purchase of capital assets.

Deferred Capital Contributions
Deferred capital contributions represent the unamortized amount of donations and grants received for the purchase of capital assets. The amortization of capital contributions is recorded as revenue in the statement of operations.

Endowments
Endowments include restricted donations received by the Organization and donations internally designated by the Board of Directors. Investment returns generated from endowments are used in accordance with the various purposes established by the donors or by the Board of Directors. The Organization protects the future purchasing power of its endowments by capitalizing a portion of the annual investment income earned. Furthermore, the Organization has established a policy of setting the amount of income available for spending at 5% of the endowment.

Endowments

Net assets restricted for endowments consist of externally restricted donations received by the Organization and internal resources transferred by the Board. In such cases, the Board has the right to subsequently remove the designation. In either instance, the endowment principal must remain intact. The investment income generated from endowments must be used in accordance with the various purpose established by donors or the Board. As part of its fiduciary responsibilities, the Organization ensures that all funds received with a restricted purpose are expended for that purpose.

Endowed Funds

The endowment funds are subdivided into appropriated net asset classifications. The permanently restricted endowment funds represent gifts where the donor has stipulated that the principal is not to be expensed. Temporarily restricted and unrestricted endowment funds represent donations where there is no requirement to maintain principal.

Endowment Funds

The endowment fund represents donations provided by benefactors or funds designated by the Board, which are restricted as to purpose and expendability. Only income earned and not designated to provide for inflation protection and growth may be expended on the designated purpose. Endowment earnings available for expenditure are recorded in the Research and Trust Fund.

Foreign Exchange Translation

The Organization accounts for transactions in a foreign currency at the exchange rate in effect at the date of the transaction. At year-end, monetary assets and liabilities denominated in a foreign currency are translated at year-end exchange rates and any translation gain or loss is included in operations. Foreign exchange gains and losses have been included in investment income.

Fund Raising Activities

Gifts and grants from fund raising activities are recorded when received. Pledges are recorded when paid.

Fund Raising Activities

Gifts and grants from fund raising activities are recorded when received. Pledges are recorded upon payment. Expenses incurred for fund raising campaigns are amortized over the length of the campaign.

Internal Restrictions

The Organization restricts a portion of its operating net assets for specific future uses. When incurred, related expenses are charged to operations and the balance of internally restricted assets is reduced accordingly.

Inventory Valuation

Inventories are reported at the lower of cost or net realizable value.

Inventory Valuation

Inventories are valued at the most recent purchase price. The costs of in stock items are adjusted to reflect the cost of the most recent purchase. Provision is made for obsolescence. This method of valuation does not result in amounts that are significantly different from actual costs.

Investments
Investments are stated at cost or, when donated, at fair market value at date of receipt, plus accrued interest. Gains on sales of investments are recorded in the year of disposal and are included in income from investments. Losses are recognized in the year of disposal or when there is a significant and permanent impairment in value. Incurred losses are netted with income from investments.

Funds are generally pooled and either managed by external fund managers or maintained as working capital and invested in fixed income investments.

Investments
Short-term and long-term investments are recorded at cost or, where donated, at fair market value on the date of receipt. Gains and losses on sales of investments are recognized in the year of disposal and are included in investment income.

Investments
Cash and short-term investments include cash and liquid investments with maturity dates ranging from two months to five years. Due to the short period to maturity, the cost of these investments is reported at fair market value.

Long-term investments consist of pooled funds. Investments are distributed among several classes of assets in order to reduce exposure to investment volatility risk.

Investments
Short-term investments are recorded at the lower of cost and market value. Investments in fixed securities, that are to be held to maturity, are recorded at cost plus accrued interest. Other investments are recorded at market value. Unrealized gains (losses) are included in investment income. Externally restricted investment income is recognized as revenue when related expenses are incurred. Externally restricted investment income for endowments is recognized as a direct increase in net assets. Internally restricted investment income is recorded as a transfer from unrestricted to internally restricted net assets in the Statement of Changes in Net Assets. Unrestricted investment income is recognized as revenue in the year it is earned.

Investments
Investments are accounted for at cost. Where there is deemed to be a permanent impairment in value, investments are recorded at cost less amounts written off.

Gains or losses on the sale of fixed income investments are deducted or added to the book value of investments and amortized over the average maturity of securities sold.

The market value of publicly traded bonds and equities are determined based on quoted market values. The market values of unlisted or infrequently traded securities are based on quoted market yields or comparable security prices as appropriate. The real estate market values represent estimated year-end market values based on periodic cyclical appraisals by accredited appraisers.

Measurement Estimates
The preparation of financial statements in conformity with generally accepted accounting principles requires management to make estimates and assumptions that affect the amount of assets, liabilities, revenues and expenses reported in the financial statements. Actual results could differ from those estimates.

Net Assets

Net assets are classified as follows:

(a) Unrestricted Net Assets: General funds available for future operations or, if negative, cumulative operating deficit.
(b) Reserves: Funds allocated for specific purposes and unexpended budgets carried forward for future expenditures within budget units.
(c) Investments in Capital Assets: Internally generated funds invested in capital assets, exclusive of capital assets financed through long-term debt or capital contributions.
(d) Internally Restricted Endowments: Unrestricted donations and bequests that have been endowed by action of the Board of Directors, including unspent investment income.
(e) Externally Restricted Endowments: Non-expendable donations and bequests. Unspent investment income and expendable restricted donations and bequests are shown as deferred contributions.

Pension Plan

The actuarial valuation for the Organization's Retirement Plan as at March 31, 20xx reported that the plan was fully funded.

Pension Plan

The Organization operates a defined contribution pension plan in which it contributes a set amount to the plan in respect of individual employees, with a guaranteed minimum defined benefit. The actuarial report, effective January 31, 20xx, indicates that the guaranteed defined benefit portion of the pension plan has a surplus of $2,500,000. Contributions made by the Organization during the year amounted to approximately $1,750,000 (*include prior year comparative*).

Pension Plan

The Organization has two defined-benefit pension plans substantially covering all full-time salaried and hourly paid employees.

The pension expense for the year is based on the best estimate of the costs of benefits earned, of the interest costs of projected benefits and on the return on plan assets. Also included in the determination is the amortization of experience gains or losses and the plan's surplus or deficit over the expected average remaining service life of the employee group. Independent actuarial consultants annually determine expenses as well as required funding contributions.

Prepaid Expenses

Expenditures incurred for materials and services to be used in future periods are recorded as prepaid expenses and are recorded as expenses in the year consumed.

Purpose of the Organization

The Organization is community based. It operates programs and performs services under the name *(enter Organization's full legal name)*. The Organization is incorporated under (*enter section of appropriate legislation)* as a not-for-profit Organization and is a registered charity under the Income Tax Act.

The Organization is a not-for-profit Organization and as such, is exempt from income taxes under *(enter appropriate section)* of the Income Tax Act.

Purpose of the Organization

The Organization is a public Art Gallery located at *(enter full address)*. The Gallery was established as a corporation without share capital by an act of (*enter appropriate legislation*) and operates under the name *(enter Organization's full legal name).*

The Organization is a not-for-profit Organization and as such is exempt from income taxes under (*enter appropriate section*) of the Income Tax Act.

Reserves

The Board of Directors has approved a policy of permitting departments to carry forward unexpended budgets into the subsequent fiscal year for expenditure in that year. In addition, the Organization reserves other portions of fund balances for specific purposes approved by the Board of Directors.

Revenue Recognition

Operating grants are recognized in the period when received. Operating grants received for a future period are deferred until that future period and are reflected as deferred contributions.

Amounts received for sales of goods and services are recognized as revenue at the time the goods are delivered or the services are provided. Otherwise, these amounts are classified as unearned revenue.

Externally restricted contributions, for purposes other than endowment or the acquisition of capital assets, are deferred and recognized as revenue in the year in which the related expenses are incurred. Externally restricted amounts can only be used for the purposes designated by the contributors.

Externally restricted capital contributions are recorded as deferred contributions until the amount is invested to acquire capital assets. Amounts invested representing externally funded capital assets are then transferred to unamortized deferred capital contributions. Unamortized deferred capital contributions are recognized as revenue in the period in which the related amortization expense of the funded capital asset is recorded.

Endowment donations are recognized as a direct increase in endowment principal. The Organization has a policy to protect the economic value of the endowments whereby a portion of the income earned on the endowments is recorded as a direct increase in endowment principal.

Gifts-in-kind are recorded at fair market value on the date of their donation or at nominal value when the fair market value cannot be reasonably determined.

Revenue Recognition

The Organization follows the deferral method of accounting for contributions, which include donations and government grants. Unrestricted contributions are recognized as revenue when received or receivable, if the amount can be reasonably estimated and collection is reasonably assured. Externally restricted contributions, other than endowments, are deferred and recognized as revenue in the year in which the related expenses are recognized. Endowment contributions are recognized as direct increases in net assets in the period in which they are received. Restricted investment income is recognized as income in the year in which the related expenses are incurred. Unrestricted investment income is recognized as income when earned. All other unrestricted income, such as fees from the sale of services, is recognized as income when earned.

Statement of Cash Flow

A statement of cash flow has not been presented, as no further useful information would be provided.

Subsequent Events

In December 20xx, the Organization entered into an agreement to sell a parcel of land to REX Developers for approximately $12.5 million. The transaction closed in January 20xx, and the resulting gain of approximately $ 7 million will be recognized in the financial statements for the period ended March 31, 20xx.

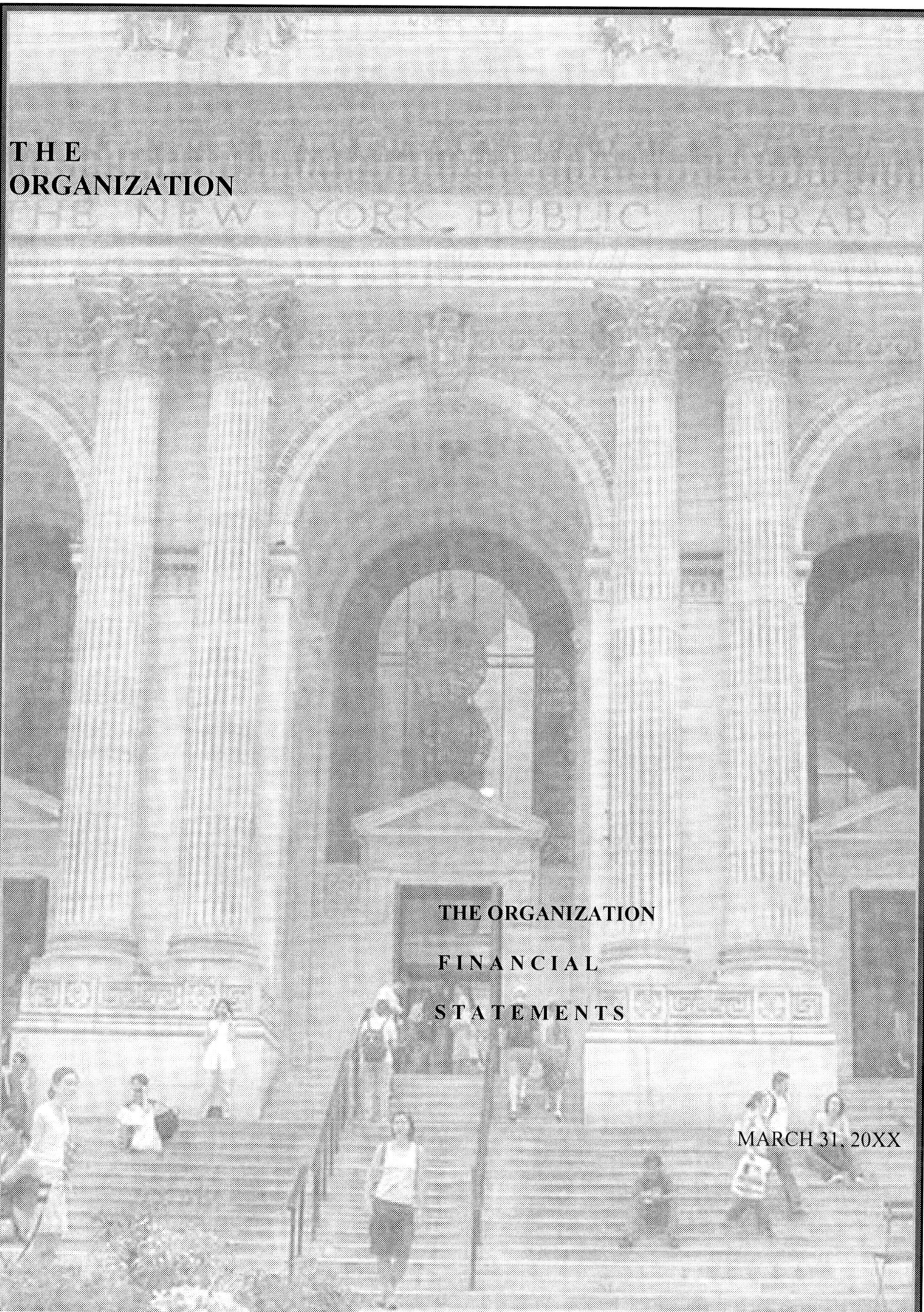

T H E
ORGANIZATION

THE ORGANIZATION

F I N A N C I A L

S T A T E M E N T S

MARCH 31, 20XX

THE ORGANIZATION
NOTES TO THE FINANCIAL STATEMENTS
For the Year Ended March 31, 20xx

1. AUTHORITY AND PURPOSE

The Organization operates as a not-for-profit entity under the authority of the *(include appropriate act of incorporation if applicable)* Act. The Organization is a registered charity and is therefore exempt from income taxes under *(include appropriate section and appropriate act).*

2. SIGNIFICANT ACCOUNTING POLICIES AND REPORTING PRACTICES

These financial statements have been prepared by management in accordance with generally accepted accounting principles as considered appropriate for not-for-profit organizations, applied consistently within the framework of the accounting policies summarized below:

(a) Fund Accounting

The accounts of the Organization are maintained in accordance with the principles of fund accounting in order to observe the limitations and restrictions placed on the use of available resources. Under fund accounting, resources for various purposes are classified for accounting and reporting purposes into separate funds in accordance with specified activities or objectives. For financial reporting purposes, the Organization has combined funds with similar characteristics into five major fund groups that are categorized as follows:

i The Operating Fund presents the administrative and other operating activities of the Organization.

ii The Capital Fund presents the funds received and expended on property, plant and equipment. It excludes the capital expenditures related to ancillary enterprises, however, which maintain their own capital ledgers.

iii The Ancillary Enterprises Fund presents the operations of services carried on by the Organization that are supportive of, but not directly related to the Organization's primary function. Any deficit incurred by an Ancillary is recoverable from its future earnings. The Ancillary Enterprises Fund includes the following:

(a) Cafeteria Services
(b) Laundry Services
(c) Parking Services

iv The Trust Fund includes those funds provided by benefactors and external contracts, the expenditure of which is restricted to a specific purpose or purposes. Also included are earnings on endowments available for expenditure.

v The Endowment Fund presents donations provided by benefactors or funds designated by the Board of Directors, which are restricted as to purpose and expendability. Only income earned and not designated to provide for inflation protection and growth may be expended on the designated purpose. Endowment earnings available for expenditure are recorded in the Trust Fund.

(b) Investments

The Organization reports its investments at the lower of cost or market.

(c) Financial Instruments

Accounts receivables are recorded at estimated net realizable value, which approximates fair value. Accounts payable and long-term debt is recorded at their cost amounts, which approximates fair value.

(d) Inventory Valuation

Inventories are recorded at the lower of cost or market.

(e) Capital Assets

Capital assets are recorded at cost less accumulated amortization. The cost of capital assets is amortized on a straight-line basis over their estimated useful life as follows:

Land Improvements	50 years
Buildings	40 years
Furniture and Equipment	10 years

(f) Internal Financing

The Organization follows a practice of making temporary advances to operating departments and other funds in order to finance the acquisition of certain capital assets. Interest charged on internal loans is recorded in the revenues of the lending fund and the expenses in the borrowing fund. The outstanding balance of these loans has been disclosed by fund.

(g) Leases Payable

The Organization has entered into certain equipment and building leases for which title to the related assets will vest in the Organization on the termination of the lease. The cost of these assets is reflected in capital assets and the present value of the lease commitments is reflected as a liability.

(h) Appropriations of Fund Balances

Appropriations are restrictions of fund balances designated for future purchase order commitments, capital and renovation projects committed but not completed, unspent organizational unit funds permitted to be carried forward at the end of each fiscal year for expenditure in the following fiscal year, or contingencies, in such amounts as are deemed necessary by the Board of Directors.

(i) Recognition of Revenue

The Organization accounts for restricted contributions in accordance with the deferral method.

Contributions restricted for the purposes other than endowment or the acquisition of capital assets are deferred and recognized as revenue in the year in which the related expenses are incurred.

Contributions restricted to the acquisition of capital assets having limited life are initially recorded as deferred contributions in the period in which they are received. They are recognized as revenue over the useful life of the related assets.

Restricted contributions for unlimited life assets, such as land, are recognized as direct increases in net assets in the period in which they are received.

Endowment contributions and related investment income, allocated for endowment capital preservation and growth, are recognized as direct increases in net assets in the period in which they are received or earned.

Unrestricted contributions are recognized as revenue when received.

Revenue received for the provision of goods and services are recognized in the period in which the goods or services are provided by the Organization. Revenues received for a future period are deferred until the goods or services are provided.

(j) Pension Plan

The Organization maintains a defined pension plan for its employees. Pension plan assets, liabilities and changes in the net assets are reported in the financial statement of the plan. The assets of the plan are held by an independent custodian and are not recorded in the accounts of the Organization. Recorded in the Organization's statements is the actuarially determined cost of maintaining this plan. The accumulated difference between this cost and the Organization's funding contribution has been reflected in the Organization's statement as a deferred pension asset.

The actuarially determined present value of accrued pension benefits for the Organization's defined pension plan as of March 31, 20xx was $50,000,000 (*include prior year comparative*).

(k) Post Retirement Benefits

The Organization provides extended health care and dental plan benefits to retirees and their eligible dependents on a cost-share basis. The Organization's share of these costs *(20xx, $1,000,000 also include prior year comparative)* is expensed in the period in which they are paid.

3. CHANGES IN ACCOUNTING POLICY AND PRESENTATION PRACTICE

Revenue Recognition

In prior years, revenue was recognized on the accrual basis with the exception of pledges and trust fund benefactions that were accounted for on a cash basis. During the year, the Organization changed to the accounting policy described in Note 2 (i).

4. INTERFUND

Included in the interfund balance is temporary financing advanced from non-endowed trust funds to other funds and departments. Interfund interest is charged on these loans using rates based on long term financing costs that are reviewed annually. These loans will be repaid from future revenues according to approved repayment schedules.

[In thousands of dollars]	TRUST FUND	CAPITAL FUND	ANCILLARY FUND
Internal Loans			
Beginning Balance	20,500	(17,000)	(3,500)
Advances	1,000	(1,000)	
Repayments	(1,000)	500	500
Ending Balance	20,500	(17,500)	(3,000)

5. INVESTMENTS

Funds are invested in a diversified-pooled fund of domestic equities, bonds, foreign equities and cash investments. Investments are reported at cost.

	BOOK VALUE		MARKET VALUE	
[In thousands of dollars]	20xx	20xx	20xx	20xx
Ancillary Enterprises Investments				
Cash and Short Term Notes	2,500	3,000	3,000	6,500
Guaranteed Investment Certificates	1,000	750	1,060	3,000
Federal Government Bonds	3,000	2,250	3,200	
	6,500	6,000	7,260	9,500
Trust Fund Investments				
Federal Government Bonds	700	725	700	750
Endowed Fund Investments				
Guaranteed Investment Certificates	50	45	55	45
Federal Government Bonds	75	70	75	70
Municipal Debentures	350	375	375	360
	475	490	505	475
Total Investments	7,675	7,215	8,465	10,725

6. INVESTMENT INCOME

[In thousands of dollars]	Operating	Ancillary Enterprises	Trust	Endowment	20xx	20xx
Realized Investment Income	1,800	180	2,000	3,000	6,980	6,500
Unrealized Investment Income		300	1,000	2,000	3,300	3,000
Total Investment Income	1,800	480	3,000	5,000	10,280	9,500
Investment Income Endowed				(1,000)	(1,000)	(2,000)
Income Available for Expenditure			4,000	(4,000)		
Net change in Deferred Contributions			(2,000)		(2,000)	(1,500)
Total Net Investment Income	1,800	480	5,000	0	7,380	6,000

7. CAPITAL ASSETS

(a) Capital Fund

[In thousands of dollars]	Cost	20XX Accumulated Amortization	Net Book Value	20XX Net Book Value
Land	1,000		1,000	1,000
Land Improvements	5,000	1,250	3,750	3,850
Buildings	25,000	8,000	17,000	17,625
Furniture and Equipment	2,000	1,000	1,000	1,200
Construction In Progress	1,500		1,500	500
	34,500	10,250	24,250	24,175

(b) Ancillary Enterprises

[In thousands of dollars]	Cost	20XX Accumulated Amortization	Net Book Value	20XX Net Book Value
Land	250		250	250
Land Improvements	150	50	100	100
Buildings	1,000	100	900	925
Furniture and Equipment	500	100	400	450
Construction In Progress	50		50	
	1,950	250	1,700	1,725

(c) Insured Values

[In thousands of dollars]	20XX Net Book Value	20XX Insured Value
Buildings	17,900	30,000
Furniture and Equipment	1,400	2,500
	19,300	32,500

8. DEBT LONG TERM

[In thousands of dollars]	Payment Frequency	Interest Rate	Annual Payment Amount	Due Date	Total March 31, 20XX	Total March 31, 20XX
Leases Payable						
Royal Trust	Monthly	5.50	50	Jan. 1, 20aa	740	750
Credit International	Monthly	7.25	65	Jun. 7, 20bb	650	685
Xerox Corporation	Monthly	7.00	10	May 5, 20cc	55	60
Xerox Corporation	Monthly	7.00	8	Feb. 2, 20dd	40	45
The IBM Corporation	Quarterly	5.50	100	Mar. 1, 20ee	400	475
Total Leases Payable					1,885	2,015
Mortgages Payable						
Royal Trust	Monthly	5.00	15	Mar. 1, 20aa	150	155
The Peoples Bank	Monthly	5.50	18	May 1, 20bb	200	205
Manulife Bank	Monthly	6.00	20	July 1, 20cc	150	160
Total Mortgages Payable					500	520
Leases and Mortgages Payable					2,385	2,535
Current Portion					(160)	(150)
Long Term Debt Payable					2,225	2,385

Note: The annual payment amounts reported above include both interest and principal.

The cash needed to satisfy the Organization's current Lease and Mortgage liability in the next five years is summarized as follows:

[In thousands of dollars]	Principal Payment	Interest Payment	Total Payment
March 31, 20aa	175	111	286
March 31, 20bb	190	96	286
March 31, 20cc	210	76	286
March 31, 20dd	135	51	186
March 31, 20ee	156	30	186
	866	364	1,230

Thereafter total payments amount to $5,500.

9. DEFERRED REVENUE, CONTRIBUTIONS AND CAPITAL CONTRIBUTIONS

[In thousands of dollars]	Operating Fund	Capital Fund	$ Ancillary Enterprise	Trust Fund	Total March 31, 20XX	Total March 31, 20XX
(a) Deferred Revenue						
Prepaid Leases, Fees and Grants	125		200		325	350
Other	75		50		125	140
	200		250		450	490
Less: Current Deferred Revenue	(200)		(55)		(255)	(300)
	0		195		195	190
(b) Deferred Contributions						
Balance, beginning of year		600		995	1,595	1,410
Contributions received during year				60	60	55
Income earned on funds				20	20	15
Contributions taken into income		(75)		(55)	(130)	(115)
Balance, end of year		525		1,020	1,545	1,365
(c) Deferred Capital Contributions						
Balance, beginning of year		1,250	500		1,750	1,690
Contributions received during year		65	35		100	70
Amortization of deferred capital contributions		(70)	(20)		(90)	(90)
Balance, end of year		1,245	515		1,760	1,670
Total of Deferred Revenue, Contributions and Capital Contributions	0	1,770	710	1,020	3,500	3,225

10. INTERFUND TRANSACTIONS

[In thousands of dollars]	Operating Fund	Capital Fund	Ancillary Enterprises	Trust Fund	Endowment Fund
Repairs and Renovations	(500)	1,000	(250)	(250)	
Capital Equipment	(100)	500	(300)	(100)	
Transfer from Ancillaries			(150)		150
Other Transactions	(350)	400	100	(150)	
	(950)	1,900	(600)	(500)	150

11. SALARY DISCLOSURE

In accordance with the Public Sector Disclosure Act (*enter appropriate section and act if regulation applies to your jurisdiction)* all salaries and benefits paid in respect of employment to employees who are paid a salary of $100,000 or more in a calendar year are listed below:

Employee	Position Title	Annual Salary	Taxable Benefits
Samantha Butler	Executive Director	125,000	1,500
Jordan Campbell	Chief Financial Officer	120,000	1,250
Ryan Martin	Director Physical Resources	120,000	1,000
Clare Rife	Director Computer Services	110,000	750
Manny Walsh	Director Ancillary Enterprises	105,000	3,000

Taxable Benefits include insurance, subsidized meals and employer owned automobile.

12. COMMITMENTS

Costs to complete major capital projects in progress as at March 31, 20XX are estimated to be $1,000,000 (20XX $1,250,000 *comparative amount*) and will be funded by government grants, donations and the resources earned by the Organization.

13. CONTINGENCY

The Organization is currently a defendant in a legal proceeding. The claim against the Organization in this proceeding has not been reflected in these financial statements. It is the opinion of management, the Organization's legal counsel and its auditors that the resolution of this claim will not have a material effect on the financial position of the Organization.

Section III (a)

PROPERTY MANAGEMENT AGREEMENT

INTRODUCTION TO A PROPERTY MANAGEMENT AGREEMENT

Revenue earned from real property is often the main source of funding for many not-for-profit Organizations. It is therefore essential to have this asset managed well. One of the first steps towards good management and profitability is selecting a reputable property management firm. Once selected, a well-defined Property Management Agreement will provide that property management firm with clear expectations and direction.

The generic document that follows is but one example of a well-written Property Management Agreement. It is inclusive, key terms are well defined lessening the chance of ambiguity, and the overall use of common language makes it easy to read and understand.

As this is a generic Agreement there are likely articles in it that do not pertain to your Organization. These articles should be ignored. Conversely, if there is a missing article then you need to add it.

A good Property Management Agreement should cover all current and potential events that have an impact, or will likely have an impact, on the Organization's real property.

The Agreement should be unique to the Organization for which it is written.

Helpful Hints:

- Your Property Management Agreement should form part of the tendering package when looking to hire a property management firm.
- The Organization's lawyer should review the Agreement.
- Before the Agreement is signed, all parties should meet to review the document, article by article.
- The property committee of the Board of Directors, in conjunction with the staff person who is most familiar with the building, should review the Property Management Agreement annually.
- If significant and on going events occur that are not identified in the articles of the Agreement, then in concurrence with the property manager, the original Agreement should be amended.

PROPERTY MANAGEMENT AGREEMENT

This Agreement was made as of the *day, month, and year.*

BETWEEN:

Hereinafter called the 'OWNER'

AND:

Hereinafter called the 'MANAGER'

WHEREAS the Owner is the registered owner of the lands and buildings described in **Schedule 1** *(attached)*, which premises are to be operated by the Owner, on a 'not-for-profit' basis;

AND WHEREAS the Owner has agreed to appoint the Manager as manager of the Portfolio for the term set out herein;

AND WHEREAS the Manager has agreed to accept such appointment on the terms and conditions as set out in this agreement;

IN CONSIDERATION of the mutual covenants contained herein, the parties agree as follows:

ARTICLE 1 DEFINITIONS
For the purpose of this Agreement, the following terms shall, unless the content requires otherwise, have the meanings specified in this article:

1.1 'AGREEMENT' shall mean this agreement and all schedules, including supplemental and amending agreements and/or addenda herein properly executed to supplement or amend this Agreement.

1.2 'BOARD' shall mean the Board of Directors of the Owner.

1.3 'EFFECTIVE DATE' shall mean the first day of (*include appropriate day, month and year).*

1.4 'MANAGER' shall mean the management/operational services agent and its employees.

1.5 'DEPARTMENT' shall mean the *(enter appropriate legislative jurisdiction)* as represented by the Department of (*enter appropriate authority)* or its successors.

1.6 'OPERATING BUDGET' shall mean the operating budget for the Portfolio as approved by the Department of *(enter appropriate authority).*

1.7 'PORTFOLIO' shall mean the lands described in the attached **Schedule 1** together with the residential rental accommodation and other structures, chattels and improvements erected or contained therein and all lands hereafter acquired by the Owner in substitution for, or in addition to, the lands described in **Schedule 1**.

1.8 'SCHEDULES' shall mean the following attached schedules (as amended or replaced from time to time) that form an integral part of this Agreement:

Schedule 1 Description of the Portfolio
Schedule 2 Conflict of Interest Directive

ARTICLE 2 THE MANAGER

2.1 The Manager acknowledges that it is familiar with the Portfolio and is fully aware of and understands all requirements and provisions of this agreement.

2.2 The Manager represents and warrants that it is an experienced and competent manager of projects similar to the Portfolio and that it has the necessary experience, qualifications and employees to manage such a Portfolio.

2.3 The Owner agrees to retain the manager and the Manager agrees to serve the Owner, as his/her exclusive agent, and to manage the Portfolio on behalf of the Owner in a faithful, diligent and honest manner, subject always to the direction of the Board, and in accordance with the terms of this agreement and all applicable By-laws, laws, regulations or ordinances of all competent authorities having jurisdiction over the Portfolio.

ARTICLE 3 MANAGER'S SERVICES - STAFFING AND CONTRACTS

Without limiting the generality of the foregoing, the Manager shall exercise the following powers, duties, discretions, rights and authorities related to staffing and contracts:

3.1 Provide, or cause to be provided, competent personnel for operating, maintaining, leasing, controlling and managing the Portfolio as would a reasonable and prudent owner of residential investment properties comparable in age, type and class to the properties of the Portfolio. The Manager agrees that such employees, servants, own agents or sub-contractors as the case may be, so engaged in the performance of this Agreement, are hired and dismissed solely by the Manager and shall be the employees, servants, own agents or subcontractors of the Manager and not employees of the Owner. All costs damages and/or severance shall be the Manager's sole responsibility;

3.2 Hire, in conjunction with the Owner, the services of full-time superintendents. Upon the hiring of such building personnel by the Owner, supervise, on behalf of the Owner, such personnel, maintain accurate payroll records with respect to such personnel in the name of the Owner, issue payment of salaries for such personnel out of the Operating Account on behalf of and in the name of the Owner, prepare such reports as required by law and withhold and remit, on behalf of the Owner, any amounts (including without limitation Income Tax, Federal Pension Plan, Employment Insurance and Employer Health Tax) required by law, and arrange on behalf of and in the name of the Owner, as employer, under the Workers' Compensation Act. All such building personnel are, and shall be at all times, employees of the Owner and not the Manager and by execution of this Agreement, the Owner assumes all employer liabilities with respect to such personnel and all salaries, benefits and other employee payments shall be the responsibility of the Owner; and

3.3 Retain the services of such experts and consultants as may be necessary from time to time, having first obtained the Owner's approval in writing and at the Owner's expense, for the proper maintenance and management of the Portfolio subject to the approved operating budget and Department approvals.

ARTICLE 4 MANAGER'S SERVICES - APPLICANTS AND TENANTS

In addition, the Manager shall exercise the following powers, duties, discretion, rights and authorities related to applicants and tenants:

4.1 Receive and record all applications for rental in the Owner's Portfolio and ensure all information on the application forms is maintained on a separate waiting list specifically for the Owner, which waiting list shall be maintained in a current and timely fashion according to the Operating Agreement and any applicable Department directives;

4.2 Take all reasonable steps to maintain full occupancy of the units, both market and rent-geared-to-income, contained in the Portfolio, including but not limited to, advertising the availability of units for rental, from time to time, and to provide such services as may be necessary to prepare the Portfolio or any part thereof for lease-up;

4.3 Verify the income and calculate the rents of all rent-geared-to-income tenants not less frequently than every 12 months and upon request of the tenant in accordance with the Operating Agreement, making such adjustments in the rents as shall be required;

4.4 Review the market rents for the Portfolio not less frequently than once a year and present a recommendation of proposed rents to the Owner for approval;

4.5 List, offer for lease and enter into, on behalf of the owner, all leases, renewals of leases, extensions and termination of leases on such terms as are customary for dwelling units similar to the dwelling units of the Portfolio and in conformity with the rental policy of the Owner and the Department as set forth in the Operating Agreement;

4.6 Demand, sue for, enforce payment, receive and give receipts and discharges for rent and other monies becoming due in respect of the Portfolio, subject to the arrears and collections policies set by the Owner;
4.7 Commence, carry on, prosecute to judgment and defend all actions and other proceedings relating to the Portfolio, having first obtained the Owner's approval and instructions;

4.8 Settle or submit for collection or arbitration, if applicable, all accounts, claims and disputes in respect of such rents and other monies, having first obtained the Owner's instructions; and

4.9 Supervise the moving in and moving out of tenants of the Portfolio so as to result in a minimum of disturbance to the Portfolio or inconvenience to the tenants thereof.

ARTICLE 5 MANAGER'S SERVICES - MAINTENANCE

Additionally, the Manager shall exercise the following powers, duties, discretion, rights and authorities in relation to the maintenance of the Portfolio:

5.1 Keep and maintain the Portfolio in a state of cleanliness as would a prudent owner of a well maintained dwelling comparable in type, age, class and location to the Portfolio and purchase all necessary cleaning materials and other supplies required for this purpose within the approved Operating Budget and at the owner's expense;

5.2 Adequately maintain and care for the landscaping, snow removal and garbage disposal of the Portfolio. All services contemplated herein shall be at the expense of the owner and subject to the limitations of the approved operating budget;

5.3 Carry out monthly physical inspections of the Portfolio and make or arrange for all necessary repairs or alterations to the buildings, grounds and equipment in the Portfolio, including the maintenance, repair and replacement of appliances or the heating, plumbing and electrical equipment as may be deemed necessary or desirable for its efficient management or operations or to improve the rentability thereof, including those repairs or alterations necessary so as to comply with any and all regulations of the Health Unit, Police and Fire Departments or any other Municipal, State or Federal authority having jurisdiction over the Portfolio, subject to the qualifications contained herein. All services, excluding the physical inspections conducted by the Manager, contemplated herein shall be at the expense of the Owner and subject to the limitations of the approved operating budget; and

5.4 Arrange for and keep the Portfolio heated to a reasonable temperature and operate and maintain the heating equipment in accordance with the Owner's obligations to its tenants.

ARTICLE 6 MANAGER'S SERVICES - FINANCIAL MANAGEMENT

Additionally, the manager shall ensure the following duties and functions, related to the financial management of the Portfolio, are accurately carried out:

6.1 Maintain appropriate books of account and financial records with respect to all financial operations of the Portfolio, which books of account shall be kept in accordance with Generally Accepted Accounting Principles and shall be acceptable in form and content and accessible to the Owner, the Department and the Owner's auditors;

6.2 Pay from the Owner's accounts, and subject to the banking policy set forth herein, all mortgage payments payable, and deliver such statements and generally do all things which are or may be required to be done or performed by the Owner pursuant to the provisions of any such mortgage;

6.3 Pay from the Owner's accounts and subject to the banking policy set forth herein, all expenses, invoices and charges incurred in the operation of the Portfolio as they become due including all municipal realty taxes, rates and assessments, including local improvement rates, utility charges, advertising costs, superintendent wages, insurance premiums, heating and cooling charges, costs of repairs, maintenance, landscaping and other operating expenditures incurred in the operation of the Portfolio and not otherwise provided for in this Agreement;

6.4 Maintain, at the Owner's expense and in accordance with the Operating Agreement and requirements of the mortgagee, insurance coverage with respect to property and public liability, fire and rental loss;

6.5 Collect all rental payments and all other sums required to be paid by the tenants of the Portfolio and any other sums of any nature or kind which may be receipts due and payable in connection with or incidental to the Portfolio, including, without limiting the generality of the foregoing, any security deposits, compensation, rent, laundry and parking revenue, and deposit same into the Owner's Bank Account on the same day as collected as instructed by the Owner, and provide to the Owner such bank receipts as the Owner shall require;

6.6 Prepare and deliver annually for the Owner's approval, on or before (*enter appropriate year, month and day)* a draft Operating Budget for the following fiscal year commencing *(enter appropriate year, month and day)*;

6.7 Prepare, upon reasonable notice, for approval of the Owner and the Owner's auditors, such financial statements in such format and detail as required with respect to the Portfolio, subject to the approval of the Owner; and

6.8 Maintain and invest, subject to the direction of the Owner, the capital reserves required to be retained by the Owner pursuant to the Operating Agreement.

ARTICLE 7 MANAGER'S SERVICES – MEETINGS AND REPORTING

In addition to the foregoing, the Manager shall exercise the following powers, duties, discretion, rights and authorities:

7.1 Attend, as required by the Owner, monthly Board of Director meeting;

7.2 Provide the Owner on at least a monthly basis, such written financial data and written property management reports as the Owner may request from the Manager;

7.3 Undertake and prepare such special reports, investigations and studies as the Owner may require from time to time;

7.4 The Manager shall notify the Owner of the name and model of the Manager's computer and of the operating system and software on which it is currently operating and storing the Owner's data on a continuous basis; and

7.5 Provide informal training to the Owner as may be required.

ARTICLE 8 SPENDING AUTHORITY

8.1 All checks drawn on the Owner's bank shall be prepared by the Manager or at the direction of the Manager and shall be executed jointly by two designated signatories of the Owner.

8.2 Subject to the emergency provisions herein set forth, the Manager shall expend no funds, undertake no work or engage any contractors for maintenance or capital outlay unless the same are set forth and approved by the Owner.

8.3 In all items of maintenance, capital outlay or the engagement of consultants in excess of Five Hundred ($500.00) Dollars, the Manager shall obtain three written competitive quotations from suppliers, contractors and consultants and provide the same to the Owner together with his/her recommendations prior to engaging a contractor or a consultant or purchasing materials and supplies subject to the limitations of the approved Operating Budget and the Operating Agreement.

8.4 For contracts exceeding Fourteen Thousand Nine Hundred and Ninety Nine ($14,999) Dollars, the Manager will ensure that a public or invitational tender is implemented in accordance with the Owner's approval.

8.5 If a situation arises that in the opinion of the Manager constitutes an emergency, the Manager may take such steps as are required to react to and rectify such emergency and expend such funds as may be necessary. Provided always that in an emergency situation, the Manager must, as soon as possible, use his/her best efforts to contact the Owner immediately and in the event of an emergency situation, the Manager shall provide a full written report to the Owner and, where necessary, the Department, within Thirty (30) Days outlining the emergency, the steps taken to rectify it and the expenses resulting there from.

ARTICLE 9 TERM

9.1 The Manager's appointment hereunder shall commence *(enter appropriate Month, Day, Year)* and shall run for a period of two (2) Years, with an expiry date of *(enter appropriate Month, Day, Year)*, unless terminated pursuant to the terms of this agreement.

9.2 It is hereby expressly agreed that the Owner reserves the right to cancel and terminate this agreement without cause by giving the Manager Sixty (60) days written notice of such termination. Such termination shall take effect on the last day of the month at which time accounts between the Parties shall be settled.

9.3 It is hereby expressly agreed that the Owner reserves the right to cancel and terminate this agreement with cause by giving the Manager Thirty (30) days written notice of such termination. Such termination shall take effect on the last day of the month at which time accounts between the Parties shall be settled.

9.4 Should the Owner wish to renew this Agreement, under the same or altered terms and conditions, a new agreement must be signed at least Sixty (60) days prior to the end of the term. The new term of the new agreement shall be for a period of not more than two full years.

9.5 The Manager acknowledges that there will be no automatic renewal of this agreement for a subsequent term and that the Owner has the right to tender for the services of a succeeding property manager prior to the expiration of the term herein.

ARTICLE 10 FEE

10.1 The Owner shall pay the Manager 3.5% of the Gross Residential Rental Income for the provision of the services described in this Agreement.

ARTICLE 11 INDEMNIFICATION OF MANAGER

11.1 The Owner does hereby indemnify and save the Manager harmless from and against any actions, claims, cost or expense whatsoever relating to the first or subsequent mortgages, if any, and from and against any actions, claims, costs, payments or liabilities whatsoever arising out of the use, occupation or management of the Portfolio, including injury or death to any person or damage to any property during the whole of the terms hereof, save only for such claims or liabilities arising by virtue of the Manager's or its servants', contractors', agents', or employees' negligent acts, dishonest acts or omissions. Such indemnification shall survive the expiration of the term hereof in respect to payments or liabilities suffered or incurred during the said term.

ARTICLE 12 INDEMNIFICATION OF OWNER

12.1 The Manager shall indemnify and save the Owner harmless from and against any loss, damage, expense or liability the Owner may suffer or incur by reason of the negligent acts, dishonest acts or omissions of the Manager, its agents, representatives, servants or employees. The Manager shall also indemnify and save the Owner harmless from any action, claim, demand and expense or damage the owner may suffer or incur by reason of the Manager, its servants, agents, representatives or employees exceeding their authority. The Manager warrants to the Owner that it shall be fully liable for the application of the income from the Portfolio in accordance with the provisions of this Agreement. Such indemnification shall survive the expiration of the term hereof in respect to payments or liabilities suffered or incurred during the said term.

ARTICLE 13 FIDELITY BONDS

13.1 The Manager shall provide the Owner with evidence that it maintains fidelity bonds in form, substance and amount reasonably acceptable to the Owner bonding itself, its employees, agents and contractors and indemnifying the Owner against loss, theft, embezzlement or other fraudulent acts on the part of the Manager or its employees, agents and contractors who are engaged in carrying out the services covered by this Agreement. The cost of such fidelity bonds shall be borne by the property manager.

ARTICLE 14 ASSIGNMENT

14.1 Except as expressly provided herein, this Agreement shall not be assignable by the Manager without the prior written approval of the Owner which approval may be arbitrarily withheld and the manager shall not delegate its responsibilities, rights and authorities hereunder other than to its employees and as provided herein, its contractors, servants and agents.

ARTICLE 15 NOTICES

15.1 Any notice to be given by either party to the other or any document or other instrument hereby provided or permitted shall be deemed to have been sufficiently and effectually given and/or delivered, if delivered on a business day, then on the day of delivery, or if mailed by prepaid registered post, then on the second day following the registration thereof. Either party may from time to time by notice to the other, change the address, to which notices, documents or instruments are to be given, served or delivered. The address at which the persons to whom such notices, instruments or documents are to be given, served or delivered until changed are as follows:

TO THE MANAGER: XYZ Company
123 Happy Lane
Rogersville, *(enter full mailing address)*
Attention: Joy Rogers, President
Telephone: 888-666-1234

TO THE OWNER: The Happy People
456 Start Road
Muppetland, *(enter full mailing Address)*
Attention: Executive Director
Telephone: 888-666-4455

15.2 The Owner shall furnish to the Manager from time to time as required a list showing the names, address and telephone numbers of those Officers, Directors or other representatives who are authorized to act for and on behalf of the Owner whenever the Manager elects or is required under the terms of this Agreement, to consult with the Owner and/or obtain its approval before proceeding with any work, act, or action. Wherever it is provided herein that a consent, approval or other action shall be obtained from the owner, such expression shall be deemed to include a requirement that such consent, approval or other action or refusal thereof shall be deemed to include a requirement that such consent, approval or other action or refusal thereof shall not be unreasonably delayed.

15.3 The Manager shall at all times keep the Owner and tenants advised of a telephone number or numbers at which an agent of the Manager may be reached during normal business hours. The Manager will also provide to the Owner a telephone number where it can be reached at any time day or night with respect to any emergency at the Portfolio.

ARTICLE 16 RESPONSIBILITIES AND RETURN OF DATA ON TERMINATION

16.1 Upon termination of this Agreement, at the end of term or pursuant to Article 9.2 and 9.3 of this Agreement, the Manager shall return to the Owner or the Owner's new Manager, within Ten (10) days of termination, all keys, invoices, books of account, leases, operating contracts, working papers, data and information which the Manager may have in its possession pertaining to the Portfolio, and as well on computer disk, the cost of which disk will be borne by the Owner. The Manager acknowledges and agrees that these are the sole and exclusive property of the Owner.

16.2 The Manager will be held legally responsible by the Owner for any substantial deterioration of the Portfolio through neglect, deliberate action or inaction, during any termination notice period.

ARTICLE 17 CONFLICT OF INTEREST

17.1 The Manager acknowledges that prior to executing this Agreement it was provided with a copy of the Department of Municipal Affairs and Housing Conflict of Interest Directive dated *(Month, Day, Year)* and that it has read the Directive and understands its terms. The Manager acknowledges that the Owner is obligated to comply with this Directive and to this end the Manager will be obliged to sign the Conflict of Interest Declaration from the Owner in the form attached to the Directive.

17.2 The Manager further agrees to provide such declaration as and when required by the Owner and acknowledges that any conflict of interest in contravention of the Directive will be immediately reported to the Owner. If it has been determined in accordance with the Department of Municipal Affairs and Housing Conflict of Interest Directive, or the Department has so determined that the Manager is in a conflict of interest, the Owner is entitled to terminate with cause this Agreement without any right or recourse by the Manager against the Owner or the Department.

ARTICLE 18 CONFIDENTIALITY

18.1 The Manager agrees that all of its employees and/or agents having access, by virtue of this Agreement, to materials and information regarding the individual tenant of the Owner shall treat same as confidential information not to be disclosed to third parties or used in any unauthorized way without the prior consent and knowledge of such individual tenant of the Owner in accordance with the Freedom of Information and Protection of Privacy Act of *(enter appropriate jurisdiction).*

ARTICLE 19 INUREMENT

19.1 This Agreement shall inure to the benefit of and be binding upon the respective successors and assigns of the parties hereto.

ARTICLE 20 ARBITRATION

20.1 In the case of any dispute between the parties as to the meaning of any part of this Agreement, or about a claim arising hereunder, the parties shall submit the dispute to a single arbitrator under the Arbitration Act of *(enter appropriate jurisdiction).* The arbitrator may appoint counsel and may submit to him/her disputed points of law, and the arbitrator may act upon the advice of counsel, and may apportion and charge the cost thereof between the parties hereto.

ARTICLE 21 GENERAL

21.1 A waiver of either the Owner or the Manager, as the case may be, of any breach of this Agreement by the other party shall not be considered a waiver of any other subsequent breaches of this Agreement. A failure of either the Owner or the Manager, as the case may be, to seek a remedy for any breach of this Agreement shall not be considered a waiver of such party's right to seek a remedy for any subsequent breaches of this Agreement.

21.2 If any term, covenant or condition of this Agreement be held in whole or in part invalid or unenforceable, the remainder of this Agreement shall not be affected thereby and each term, covenant and condition of this Agreement shall be separately valid and enforceable to the fullest extent permitted by law.

21.3 This Agreement shall not be modified or amended except, after approval by the Department, by instrument in writing signed by the parties hereto or by their successors and assigns.

21.4 The parties affirm that the Department of *(enter appropriate jurisdiction)* has agreed to the execution of this document.

IN WITNESS WHEREOF the parties hereto have hereunto affixed their corporate seal and respective signatures by the hands of their proper authorized signing officers.

EXECUTED ON BEHALF OF THE OWNER this *(enter appropriate **day, month, and year).***

We have authority to bind the Owner.

PER: ______________________ ______________________
Signature Title

PER: ______________________ ______________________
Signature Title

EXECUTED ON BEHALF OF THE MANAGER this *(enter appropriate **day, month, and year.***

We have authority to bind the Manager.

PER: ______________________ ______________________
Signature Title

PER: ______________________ ______________________
Signature Title

SCHEDULE 1
DESCRIPTION OF THE PORTFOLIO

HAPPY VILLA
456 START ROAD, MUPPETLAND

Building and Site

This apartment building, known as **Happy Villa**, is primarily a residential use building. 25 of the 75 units are retrofitted to accommodate the needs of adults with a physical disability. The building consists of seven stories with one level below grade, referred to as the lower level.

Currently its owners, **The Happy People**, provide 24-hour attendant care services to 22 adults with a physical disability. These services are non-medical and consist of assistance with activities of daily living, such as, dressing, bathing, transfers and meal assistance.

The Happy People offices, an attendant care lounge, laundry facility, storage space and the superintendent apartment occupy the lower level of the building.

The Portfolio also includes a two-level open-air garage that can house approximately 100 vehicles. The open-air garage is located on the south side of the site. The open-air garage is not directly attached to the building proper, however, access is provided from both the upper and lower decks to the building rear entrance doors.

The building cladding system generally consists of a clay brick mason veneer, supported by steel shelf angles fastened to the floor slab edges. The Building is also comprised of fixed thermal window units as well as double single-glazed horizontal slide windows and balcony doors. Balconies that extend for the entire height of the building also form the building façade.

The site elements generally consist of asphalt-paved roadways, vehicle surface parking, poured concrete curbs and sidewalks, landscaped areas and a child playground. The main access to the site is via a two-way driveway off the south side of Start Road located at the northeast quadrant of the site.

SCHEDULE 1
DESCRIPTION OF THE PORTFOLIO

HAPPY VILLA
456 START ROAD, MUPPETLAND

Mechanical and Electrical Systems

Happy Villa is serviced by gas, water, sewer and hydro systems.

The site has in-suite wall sleeves for portable air conditioning units. Site heating consists of electrical baseboard radiators individually controlled by wall-mounted thermostats.

Two Acme 402 Air rooftop units, which are individually equipped with a gas-fired heater, provide ventilation and air makeup. The building's hot water is supplied by 3 Heat Maker series J Boilers. An Arco water softener is located in the North West corner of the basement in the mechanical room. Both hot and cold water is conditioned prior to use.

Site fire protection consists of a fire standpipe and an automatic sprinkler system that is integrated into a central fire alarm. The central emergency communication system is located at the building's main entrance. Alarms are also sounded by horns that are located in each suite. The emergency diesel-powered generator is located in the mechanical room.

One garbage room services the building. The room is on the ground floor and contains a single Colt 18 garbage compactor that collects the refuse from a single garbage chute.

The building is serviced by one elevator shaft housing 2 cabs. The elevator machine room is located on the roof in a mechanical room.

Capital Renovations[1]

The Happy People received funding from the Department of Municipal Affairs and Housing to inspect and where necessary repair vertical and horizontal control joints and to replace shelf angles. This work began in *(month, year)* and was completed in *(month, year)* and brought the building up to current construction standards.

Additional funding has been sought from the Department of Municipal Affairs and Housing. If approved, the funding will be used to restore the two-level open-air parking garage, replace the 3 Heat Maker series J Boilers and retrofit the building emergency lighting system. Construction would begin on or about *(month, year)* and would end on or about *(month, year)*.

---

[1] the details of any major repair or renovation project completed in the immediate past, or any major repair or renovation project planned for the near future, should be reported as part of this Schedule.

SCHEDULE 2
CONFLICT OF INTEREST DIRECTIVE

The following is a summary of a Department Conflict of Interest Directive issued to non-profit housing providers.

1. A conflict of interest is defined as a situation where the personal or business interest of a party is in conflict with the best interest of the housing provider. A conflict of interest may occur when a party, or one of its family members, gives or receives a direct or indirect personal gain or benefit, or a direct or indirect advantage or privilege.

2. While a conflict of interest may not exist, someone might perceive that a conflict of interest exists. The test question for a perceived conflict of interest is, "would an informed person, having thought the situation through, think it possible that a party might be adversely influenced in the performance of his/her duties for the housing provider by his/her other interests?"

3. A housing provider must closely monitor its relationships, arrangements, contracts and agreements, and not engage in any activity that may result in a conflict of interest. To this end, the housing provider must obtain a Conflict of Interest Declaration in an approved form from each member of its Board of Directors, its staff and every party with which the housing provider intents to enter into a relationship, arrangement, contract or an agreement with an annual value of $14,999 or $20 per unit of housing owned by the provider, whichever is the lesser. Declarations must be retained on file for a minimum of five years from the date of signing.

4. The housing provider must promote fair and objective business practices by requiring at least three public tenders, invitational qualification tenders, or written quotations for any service or product, depending on its value; and hold an open and documented competition when hiring.

5. The housing provider must ensure that parties with whom it deals with are made aware of the *(enter appropriate Department)* Directive and the housing providers obligation to declare and to report to the Department, in the manner specified in the Directive, any conflict of interest or perceived conflicts of interest when it occurs.

6. If there are any unreported or unresolved conflicts of interest, the *(enter appropriate Department or agency)* may take action as specified in the Conflict of Interest Directive.

7. Prohibited conflicts of interest include doing business with or hiring Board members or their relatives.

8. Where greater detail, definitions, procedures, examples of conflicts, potential resolution of conflicts and other such information are required, refer to the Department of Conflict of Interest Directive for housing providers (*enter appropriate document dated day, month, year).*

Section III (b)

SUPERINTENDENT AGREEMENT

INTRODUCTION TO A SUPERINTENDENT AGREEMENT

The sample Superintendent Agreement that follows assumes that the superintendent is the employee of the not-for-profit Organization and not the Property Manager. The Agreement also assumes that the building is a rent-geared-to-income property in which 30 units are accessible for the physically challenged. In this example the employer, the not-for-profit Organization, also occupies space in the Lower Level of the building.

When reading the Agreement you will notice that much of the material is unique to the Organization for which it was written. Such Agreements by their very nature need to be specific. Any Organization that undertakes the task of either writing their first ever Agreement, or updating their old one needs to invest the time to make it unique.

Tenants, visitors and passers-by see a building as an extension of its owner. A building that is clean and well maintained will, therefore, reflect positively on the owner. A cluttered building and one in disrepair will do the opposite. This association should not be over looked or under estimated.

A well-written Superintendent Agreement and a hard working superintendent, who knows exactly what is required from him/her, are both essentials for success in operating a commercial building.

Helpful Hints:

- If you are writing the first ever Superintendent Agreement for your Organization then track down at least three other Agreements before you start. The more samples you have to draw from, the more successful you are likely to be in writing your own.

- The Organization's lawyer should review the Agreement.

- A copy of the Agreement should be provided, not less than five days prior to the interview, to each candidate you intend to interview for the superintendent's position.

- Your Superintendent Agreement should be reviewed, clause by clause, during the interview process.

- If your superintendent is not adhering to certain parts of the Agreement then meet with the individual as soon as possible. The longer bad habits persist the more difficult they are to correct.

The property committee of the Board of Directors, in conjunction with the staff person who is most familiar with the building, should review the Agreement annually.

SUPERINTENDENT AGREEMENT

Dated this *x^{st} day of Month, Year*

BETWEEN: **The Happy People**, (herein referred to as the Landlord) and,

Mr. and Mrs. Smith, (herein referred to as the Superintendent).

1. **EMPLOYMENT:** The Landlord hereby employs the Superintendent as the resident superintendent of the apartment building located at *(enter full legal address)* and described as **HAPPY VILLA**. The Superintendent hereby accepts such employment in accordance with the terms and conditions of this Agreement.

2. **DUTIES OF SUPERINTENDENT:** The Superintendent will report directly to The Happy People and shall manage and maintain the apartment building. The duties of the Superintendent shall include all necessary and related tasks, including but not limited to the following:

   (a) Meeting with tenants and prospective tenants to handle details with respect to lease signing, renewals and terminations. Issuing and taking rental applications for vacant units from applicants and submitting applications with deposit and any other documentation, as applicable, to the Landlord for final approval.
   (b) Collecting rent and any additional charges owed by the tenants and notifying tenants when rent is overdue.
   (c) Submitting all funds collected to the Landlord, for deposit, within the same month by due dates as directed by the Landlord.
   (d) Delivering rent increase notices and all communications to the tenants of the Building as required by the Landlord.
   (e) Maintaining accurate record of rents and all repairs to the Building which are to be documented on the Tenant Log for each unit or common area, which Tenant Log shall include details of unit refurbishing, unit inspections, unit repairs and all other material and relevant information regarding the unit.
   (f) Receiving tenant complaints and written requests for maintenance and taking action regarding such requests immediately or within 24 hours, dependent on the nature of the problem.
   (g) Advising tenants of infractions of the Rules and Regulations for the Building and recording details of such infractions in the Tenant Log for each applicable unit.
   (h) Providing janitorial and maintenance services, as required, to the Building, property, common areas, boardroom (including kitchen and adjacent washrooms), conference room, and grounds.
   (i) Conducting regular inspections of the Building, property and common areas; maintain general security (locked doors and windows in common areas and vacant units) and maintain lock and key records; ensure the Landlord is aware of vandalism, disturbances and tenant complaints.
   (j) Providing general maintenance and minor repairs (including lock changes and repairs, minor carpentry, minor electrical, minor plumbing repairs/maintenance and touch-up painting) that are tenant related or as directed by the Landlord.
   (k) Providing temporary emergency services and minor adjustment repairs in the common areas as required.

(l) Maintaining the grounds, landscaping, parking areas, laundry room, conference room, board-room and adjacent washrooms and all common areas on a year round basis including:

In the spring/summer/fall:

- ensuring that all lawn maintenance/fertilizing and other services which are provided by outside contractors are completed satisfactorily;
- maintaining the walkways, gardens and landscaped area (watering as necessary);
- keep the common areas and grounds clear of debris and safe for all residents and their guests;

In the winter:

- keeping all sidewalks, entrances and steps of all common areas clear of snow and ice, as required, with special concentration on wheelchair accessible areas;
- supervising the contractual snow removal services provided by outside contractors of all parking areas used by residents and their guests;

Year-round:

- supervising and maintaining general clean-up of parking areas and common areas as required;
- cleaning and maintaining laundry facilities, boardroom (including kitchen area and adjacent washrooms), conference room on a daily basis;
- cleaning inside and outside windows of lobby, and all common areas as required/requested;
- preparing for collection of garbage disposal;
- providing maintenance of compactor and washing and deodorizing of bins and compactor;
- maintaining all garbage chute rooms including deodorizing of chutes on regular basis;
- maintain general security of doors and windows in common areas and document and report any vandalism.

(m) Communicating with the Landlord with respect to all major repair work required.

(n) Obtaining pre-authorization for non-emergency repairs of a cost of one hundred dollars ($100.00) or more.

(o) Taking immediate action with respect to "life threatening" emergency situations and communicating with the Landlord regarding such situations as soon as possible and not later than two (2) hours after occurrence of such situations.

(p) Contacting Landlord approved contractors for major repairs which cannot be handled by the Superintendent, including obtaining repair quotes in advance of commencing work, obtaining Landlord prior approval where necessary or as directed, and overseeing all contractor work to ensure that work is completed as contracted.

(q) Attending with contractor when work or repairs are being provided in a unit with absentee tenants.

(r) Verifying that all subcontract work is completed in a satisfactory manner within the cost estimate provided and pre-authorized by the Landlord.

(s) Submitting copies of all completed work orders to the Landlord on a weekly basis.

(t) Maintaining an inventory of equipment and supplies needed in the execution of the job.

(u) Performing scheduled maintenance on all equipment, if qualified and able to do so, such maintenance to be based on manufacturers' recommendations and operating manual.

(v) Maintaining an accurate record of all inspections and preventative maintenance servicing of all equipment by sub-contractor.

(w) Scheduling and performing unit inspections including move-in and move-out inspections as required. Move-in inspections are to be performed within seventy-two (72) hours following move-in, in presence of the tenant and signed by the tenant. Move-out inspections are to be conducted on day of move-out in presence of vacating tenant.
(x) Cleaning of units following vacating by tenant, including refurbishing and preparation for occupancy by new tenant.
(y) Advising the Landlord of receipt of all written Notices to vacate as received and documenting such Notices in rental book records as maintained by the Superintendent and the Landlord.
(z) Providing 24-hour coverage of the Building at all times, unless prior written approval for absence by the Landlord is first obtained by the Superintendent. Relief superintendent coverage is to be pre-approved and pre-authorized by the Landlord.
(aa) Completing other duties and responsibilities as requested or assigned by the Landlord.

3. **SALARY:** The Landlord shall pay the Superintendent the gross sum of fourteen hundred ($1,400.00) dollars per month ($700 per person) as salary plus a taxable benefit of $200.00 per month ($100 per person), in accordance with this Agreement. Such salary to be paid on the last business day of every month, with an advance of approximately 50% of net pay payable on the 15th day of each month. Monthly remuneration is subject to review on an annual basis.

4. **APARTMENT AND OTHER BENEFITS:** The Superintendent shall be allowed to stay and reside in apartment *L1* (the "Unit"), free of rent to which the taxable benefit of $200.00 as described in item 3 above, will be applied monthly, with the terms of occupancy and use of the Unit as per the Landlord's standard Lease/Tenancy conditions. In addition, all hydro usage and one line basic residential phone service including call answer feature, are provided as part of the remuneration package. In addition, the use of a pager as provided by the Landlord. Benefits will also include a cost-plus insurance package which provides 100% reimbursement up to a maximum of $1,500.00 per annum, of dental, drugs, glasses and medical coverage, effective on the first day after completion of the first full month of employment, instead of the standard 90-day waiting period, coverage to commence *(enter month, day, year)* as authorized by The Organization. Receipts for the cost-plus benefit are to be submitted on a quarterly basis. The Superintendent will be entitled to two weeks vacation per annum.

The Superintendent expressly acknowledges that the granting of the tenancy of the Unit is provided by the Landlord to the Superintendent pursuant to the Landlord and Tenant Act (the "Act") *(enter appropriate Act)* and as such, pursuant to section of the Act *(enter appropriate section),* upon termination of this Agreement, the Superintendent will have seven (7) days from the date of termination to deliver vacant possession of the Unit and to surrender all keys for the Unit and the perimeter keys for the Building to the Landlord. The Superintendent agrees to use the Unit for residential purposes and as the Superintendent's quarters only and for no other purpose whatsoever. The Superintendent also agrees that it will not allow the Unit to be occupied or otherwise used by any parties other than the Superintendent.

The Superintendent further agrees to use the non-tenant storage area provided for business-related goods and equipment only.

5. **EXPENSES:** The Landlord will rebate to the Superintendent the one residential basic phone line charges plus all business related long-distance telephone charges incurred by the Superintendent after telephone invoices relating to the applicable long-distance charges have been submitted to the Landlord for reimbursement. Such invoices shall be remitted to the Landlord by the Superintendent on a monthly basis or as directed by the Landlord.

   The Superintendent will be provided by the Landlord with a petty cash float of one hundred dollars ($100.00), which is to be used exclusively for expenses incurred in carrying out the duties of the Superintendent as outlined above. Reimbursement for approved sundry petty cash expenses will be made on a monthly basis following submission of receipts by the Superintendent to the Landlord.

6. **HOURS OF WORK:** The Superintendent is expected to work at least forty (40) hours per week. The Superintendent shall also devote any additional time as required to perform the duties assigned in accordance with this Agreement.

7. **TERMS OF EMPLOYMENT:** The employment of the Superintendent shall begin on *(enter month, day, year)* and shall continue until *(enter month, day, year)* and for such additional periods of time as the parties mutually agree. The Superintendent acknowledges and understands that this Agreement is subject to a probationary period of ninety (90) days during which time this Agreement may be terminated by the Landlord without notice or cause. Written performance evaluations will be conducted after the 90-day probation period and on completion of year one of the term and on an annual basis thereafter.

8. **TERMINATION:** After the expiry of the probationary period provided for herein, either party may terminate this Agreement by giving fourteen (14) days written notice to the other party at the address set forth below, unless termination was for cause. All records and master keys for the Building are to be surrendered to the Landlord on termination.

9. **NOTICE:** Any notice required or permitted under this Agreement shall be in writing and shall be sufficiently given if delivered to the party or sent via registered mail to the following addresses:

   To the Superintendent: *(enter appropriate mailing address)*

   To the Landlord: *(enter appropriate mailing address)*

10. **SUPERINTENDENT'S COVENANTS:**

    (a) The Superintendent acknowledges that he/she has been advised by **The Happy People** and **ABC Property Management** that the property is a non-profit building in which 30 of the units are accessible units in the complex for physically challenged tenants who have special needs; that **The Happy People** provides 24-hour attendant care and occupies the Boardroom, Conference Room, Administration Offices and Attendant Care Offices within the Building; and that **The Happy People's** clients live independently, directing their own care but may at times have special needs.

(b) The Superintendent acknowledges that in the course of carrying out and performing his/her responsibilities under this Agreement, the Superintendent will have access to and will be entrusted with detailed confidential information concerning the Landlord, the Landlord's internal affairs and business operations, and the tenants of the Building (the "Confidential Information"). The Superintendent further acknowledges that the disclosure of any such Confidential Information to any party would be highly detrimental to the best interests of the Landlord and the tenants of the building. The Superintendent acknowledges and agrees that the right to keep information confidential constitutes propriety and personal rights that the Landlord and the tenant of the Building are entitled to protect. Accordingly, the Superintendent covenants and agrees with the Landlord that, save with the consent of the Landlord, the Superintendent will not, either during the term of this Agreement or at any time thereafter, disclose any Confidential Information to any person, other than the Landlord, nor shall the Superintendent use the Confidential Information for any purpose other than the purposes of the Landlord. The Superintendent agrees that all restrictions contained in this clause are reasonable and valid in the circumstances and that any defense to the strict enforcement thereof by the Landlord is hereby waived by the Superintendent.

(c) The Superintendent acknowledges that he/she is aware that the use of the conference and boardroom is restricted to **The Happy People** and related Organizations, and is not to be used for private functions or outside business-related interests. Use of the room is, at all times, subject to the rules and regulations as set out by **The Happy People**.

(d) The Superintendent agrees and acknowledges that all non-contractual subcontract work requires that a Landlord approved purchase/work order be obtained by the Superintendent in advance of the start of such work, unless instructions to the contrary are provided by the Landlord, to the Superintendent, in writing.

(e) The Superintendent agrees and acknowledges that the Superintendent must obtain pre-authorization from the Landlord for all repairs for which a quote in excess of one hundred dollars ($100.00) is obtained.

(f) The Superintendent acknowledges and agrees that a written pre-approval must be obtained from the Landlord if the Superintendent is to be absent from the Building. Coverage by a Relief Superintendent for weekends off and for vacation is to be pre-arranged and pre-authorized by the Landlord.

(g) The Superintendent acknowledges his/her responsibility to disclose to the Landlord all actual or perceived conflicts of interest, which may exist while fulfilling the terms of this Agreement. The Superintendent also acknowledges his/her responsibility to disclose to the Landlord in writing, on an ongoing basis, any actual or perceived conflicts of interest, which arise during the term of this Agreement. The Superintendent further agrees and acknowledges that, without limitation, the following relationships, arrangements, contracts and agreements are prohibited by the landlord as being conflicts of interest:

(i) The Superintendent cannot give any advantage or privilege to anyone when offering them housing accommodation unless permitted by the Landlord or his agent;

(ii) The Superintendent and family members of the Superintendent, may not have a direct or indirect interest in any business that provides advice and/or goods and services to the Landlord;

(iii) The Superintendent and family members of the Superintendent, may not engage in, or carry out, at, or on the Premises, any other business or commercial activity of any kind whatsoever, without the written consent of the Landlord or his agent.

(h) The Superintendent acknowledges and agrees that if required by the Landlord, the Superintendent will execute such other documents as the Landlord may reasonably require with respect to the Superintendent's obligations as defined by the conflict of interest guidelines *(enter state directive if appropriate).*

(i) The Landlord strives to promote an abuse free, trusting environment in which all persons respect one another while maximizing independence. Any act of abuse or harassment committed by or against, any person affiliated with **The Happy People** is unacceptable and such conduct will not be tolerated. The Superintendent acknowledges that it has been informed of **The Happy People** Abuse/Harassment Policy that is currently in place and that it has been provided with the details, including the background of the intent of this policy, and the procedures in place for both preventing and resolving situations that may be abusive or harassing.

11. **GOVERNING LAW:** The provisions of this Agreement shall be governed and interpreted in accordance with the laws of *(enter appropriate state.)*

12. **WAIVER:** A waiver by the Landlord of a breach of, or the failure to enforce, any provision of this Agreement shall not operate, or be construed as, a waiver or excuse of any subsequent breach.

13. **ASSIGNMENT:** Except as set out below, neither party to this Agreement shall assign the rights or obligations hereunder without the prior written consent of the other party. Notwithstanding the preceding sentence, the Landlord may assign its rights and obligations hereunder to any other company, business, or Organization with which the Landlord may merge, consolidate, transfer all or substantially all of its assets, or enter into an acquisition or reorganizing transaction. Furthermore, the Landlord may assign its rights and obligations, hereunder, to any other related entity.

14. **ACKNOWLEDGEMENT:**

(a) The Superintendent acknowledges that it has had sufficient time to review this Agreement thoroughly.

(b) The Superintendent acknowledges that it has received the most recent copy of **The Happy People** Abuse/Harassment Policy.

(c) The Superintendent has carefully read and understands the terms of this Agreement and the Superintendent's obligations hereunder.

(d) The Superintendent has been given an opportunity to obtain independent legal advice concerning the interpretation and effect of this Agreement.

(e) The Superintendent is voluntarily entering this Agreement.

IN WITNESS WHEREOF, the parties have executed this Agreement as of the date, first written above.

SUPERINTENDENT: Mr. and Mrs. Smith ________________________________

LANDLORD: The Happy People ________________________________

Section III (c)

FIRE SAFETY PLAN

INTRODUCTION TO FIRE SAFETY PLAN

If you own or manage Real Property then you should have a comprehensive updated Fire Safety Plan. In most jurisdictions this is not only common sense, it's also the law.

The Fire Safety Plan that follows carries on with The Happy People theme. The Happy People, a not-for-profit organization, was introduced at the beginning of this section. As you may recall, The Happy People own Happy Villa and have a Property Management Agreement with the XYZ Company.

When reading this Fire Safety Plan, you will notice that a number of responsibilities assigned to various members of the Fire Safety Committee overlap. This is not an error. By overlapping key responsibilities they are less likely to be missed.

The first page of this sample Safety Fire Plan includes a list of Appendices. As appendices are often lengthy and specific to a particular building, organization or jurisdiction their details are omitted. It is suffice to know that a good Fire Safety Plan should have them.

Helpful Hints:

- Work with your local Fire Department to create a Fire Safety Plan that is specific to your needs. Fire personnel are experts in this field and are always willing to help.
- Review your Fire Safety Plan with your insurance carrier.
- Ensure that all members of your Fire Safety Committee are competent and capable people who are able to handle all of the demands of their position.
- Once the Fire Safety Plan is implemented, ensure that it is maintained, updated and followed. If your Fire Safety Plan calls for 4 fire drills a year then, conduct no less then 4 fire drills a year.
- Never take the safety of the people under your care for granted.

FIRE SAFETY PLAN

INTRODUCTION

This Fire Safety Plan has been prepared for the Happy People and is specific to their property, the Happy Villa, which is located at 456 Start Road, Muppetland, (*insert appropriate state and ZIP code)*. The plan has been developed in accordance with the requirements of the appropriate Fire Codes of (*insert appropriate state)*, Regulation (*insert regulation number)*.

Regardless of how safe the design and construction of a building might be, the safety of the occupants also depends on their attitude to both fire prevention and their preparedness to take the required action in the event of a fire.

A complete copy of this Fire Safety Plan will be given to the Property Manager, the Building Superintendent and the Attendant Care Staff of the Happy People. All new tenants will receive the sections on Fire Hazards, Fire Emergency Procedures, Fire Drills and Appendix E - Audit of Human Resources.

LIST OF APPENDICES

Appendix A Summary of Fire Protection Systems
Appendix B Emergency Maintenance Schedule
Appendix C Fire Emergency Procedures
Appendix D Alternative Fire Safety Measures
Appendix E Audit of Human Resources
Appendix F Persons Requiring Physical Assistance
Appendix G Fire Alarm Sequencing
Appendix H Fire Drill Log
Appendix I Floor Plan Layout

GENERAL BUILDING LAYOUT

Happy Villa, located at 456 Start Road, Muppetland, (*insert appropriate state and ZIP code),* has the following general configuration:

Lower Level

- Storage Rooms - including a Bicycle Room
- Conference Room
- Mechanical and Electrical Rooms
- Kitchen
- Board Room and Meeting Room
- The Happy People Office
- Laundry Facilities
- The Superintendent's Apartment/Suites
- Washrooms

Ground Level
- 9 Tenant Apartments/Suites
- A Single Move-in Room
- Garbage Chute
- Lobby/Lounge
- Common Room
- Furnace Service Room
- A Single Mechanical Room and a Garbage Room
- Generator Room

Floors 2 through 7
- 12 Tenant Apartments/Suites per floor
- 1 Garbage Chute

Roof Access
- Elevator Machine Room

Detailed floor plans are included in Appendix I.

The building is equipped with a single stage Beltone fire alarm system. Fire alarm signals are transmitted to a Beltone 6000 Fire Alarm Control Panel (FACP), and then to Wemonitor, Limited (a local third party monitoring company). The FACP is located in the lower level electrical room. The remote enunciator is located on the ground level in the principal entrance vestibule area.

The principal Fire Protection Measures are summarized in Appendix A.

ORGANIZATION

To effectively implement this Fire Safety Plan and meet the requirements of the appropriate Fire Codes of (*insert appropriate state)*, a Fire Safety Committee will be established. This Committee will report to the Property Manager (XYZ Company).

The Committee will include 1 Fire Safety Director, 2 Assistant Fire Safety Directors, which will consist of the Building Superintendent and the Attendant Care Supervisor, and a Fire Warden. Each member of the Fire Safety Committee will be responsible for specific well-defined administrative functions that will be practiced on a regular basis throughout the year. In the event of an emergency, each member of the Committee will be expected to perform his/her duties as outlined by the Fire Safety Plan.

The Fire Safety Plan chain of command is as follows:

1. FIRE SAFETY DIRECTOR
   XYZ Company
   123 Happy Lane
   Rogersville, (*enter appropriate state and ZIP code)*
   Ms. Joy Rogers
   Telephone: (888) 666 - 1234
   Pager: (888) 413 - 3215

2. ASSISTANT FIRE SAFETY DIRECTOR 1
   Mr. James Smith
   456 Start Road
   Muppetland, (*enter appropriate state and ZIP code)*
   Apartment/Suite # 300
   Telephone: (888) 666 - 5875

3. ASSISTANT FIRE SAFETY DIRECTOR 2
   Ms. Janis Jones
   456 Start Road, On-call coordinator
   Muppetland, (*enter appropriate state and ZIP code)*
   Telephone - day: (888) 666 - 4399
   Telephone - night: (888) 666 - 4456
   Pager: (888) 413 - 5123

4. FIRE WARDEN
   Ms. Samantha Jordan
   456 Start Road
   Muppetland, (*enter appropriate state and ZIP code)*
   Apartment/Suite # 400
   Telephone: (888) 666 - 8557

ADMINISTRATION

(A) Fire Safety Director (Building Management)

As specified in the Fire Code of *(enter appropriate state)* the Fire Safety Director has numerous responsibilities. In particular, the Fire Safety Director must ensure that the following measures are completed and adhered to.

- Establish emergency procedures to be used in the case of a fire emergency.
- Appoint Fire Safety Directors to carryout fire safety duties.
- Train Fire Safety Directors and other building occupants so that they are aware of their responsibilities for fire safety.
- Hold fire drills in accordance with state Fire Code, incorporating emergency procedures appropriate to the building.
- Control fire hazards in the building.
- Maintain building facilities that have been provided for the safety of its occupants.
- Provide alternative safety measures during shutdown of the fire protection systems.
- Provide a means to notify the Muppetland Fire Department when the Fire Safety Plan is changed or when fire protection systems are shut down.
- Designate and train alternates to replace key personnel, such as Fire Safety Directors.
- On each floor, post and maintain emergency procedures and a floor plan layout.
- Designate a central evacuation meeting place where affected people can gather. The site must be a safe distance from the building.
- Ensure that the floor plan layout shows type and location of all fire emergency systems, such as, the location of the fire alarm control panel, fire hose cabinets, water control valves, all crossover floors and interconnections to adjacent buildings (if appropriate), and the primary and secondary exits to be used in the case of an emergency.
- Ensure that Fire Safety Directors are aware of tenants requiring assistance in a fire emergency and make provision to assist any tenant requiring assistance.

(B) Assistant Fire Safety Director 1

The Building Management of Happy Villa will appoint the Assistant Fire Safety Director 1 who will be responsible to carryout the administrative requirements of the Fire Safety Plan.

The Assistant Fire Safety Director 1 is responsible for:

- The implementation of the Fire Safety Plan, including the maintenance schedule for inspections and testing of the fire protection systems as required by the Fire Code of (*insert appropriate state)* and as summarized in Appendix B.
- Ensuring that the Assistant Fire Safety Director 2 has been selected and fully trained.
- Maintaining an up-to-date list of tenants and delivering that list to the Fire Safety Director.
- Maintaining current documents, including floor plan layouts, the location of all exits, manual pull stations, fire hose cabinets and standpipe riser valves, and delivering copies of these documents to the building's superintendent and the Attendant-Care office.
- Ensuring that fire emergency procedures, similar to those included in Appendix C, are posted in the building elevator lobby and at all exit stairs on each floor.
- Advising the fire department of any temporary shutdown of any fire protection system and to arrange for alternative measures for fire safety that is acceptable to the fire department. Alternative fire safety measures are included in Appendix D.
- Conducting fire drills as required by the Fire Safety Plan.
- Restoring the fire protection systems and fire alarm system to normal operation, as soon after an emergency condition has occurred, and is practical.
- Ensuring that in addition to keeping a complete copy of the Fire Safety Plan, the Assistant Fire Safety Director 2, also has a complete copy of the Plan.
- Ensuring that the Fire Safety Director's name, work, home and cell telephone numbers are posted in a prominent place in the Happy People office and in the superintendent's apartment/suite.
- Ensuring that the local Fire Department approves any revisions made to the Fire Safety Plan.
- Obtaining, from the Happy People, a list of all persons with physical and sensory disabilities and ensuring that the local Fire Department has a copy of the list.
- Being trained in the use of all fire equipment installed in the building.
- Ensuring that a suitable alternative is available in his/her absence.

(C) Assistant Fire Safety Director 2

A second Assistant Fire Safety Director will be appointed by the Building Manager (the Fire Safety Director) and will work in coordination with the Assistant Safety Director 1.

The responsibilities of the Assistant Fire Safety Director 2 are reported below.

- The Assistant Fire Safety Director 2 assumes the responsibilities of the Assistant Fire Director 1, for all persons under the direct care of the Happy People.
- To ensure that his/her name, work, home and cell telephone numbers are posted in a prominent place in the Happy People office.
- To conduct a head count of persons he/she is responsible for, and to report immediately to the local fire authority any missing persons, after an evacuation.

(D) Fire Warden

The Fire Warden will be appointed by the Property Manager (Fire Safety Director).

The responsibilities of the Fire Warden are as follows.

- In the event that the Assistant Fire Safety Director 1 is absent, the Fire Warden will assume the responsibilities of that position.
- To be responsible for the implementation of the Fire Safety Plan, including the maintenance schedule for inspections and testing of the fire protection systems as required by the Fire Code of (*enter appropriate state)* and as summarized in Appendix B.
- To ensure that the fire emergency procedures are posted at the building elevator lobby and at all exit stairs on each floor.
- To advise the local fire department of any temporary shutdown of any fire protection systems and to arrange for alternative measures for fire safety that are acceptable to the local fire authority.
- To conduct fire drills as outlined by the Fire Safety Plan.
- To ensure that each tenant, the Fire Safety Director and both Assistant Fire Safety Directors have a complete copy of the Fire Safety Plan.
- To ensure that the Assistant Fire Director's name, work, home and cell telephone numbers are posted in a prominent place in the Happy People office and in the apartment/suite of the building superintendent.
- To ensure that the local fire authority approves any revision to the Fire Safety Plan.
- To be trained in the use of all fire equipment installed in the building.

(E) Building Occupants

Building occupants do not have a direct responsibility in implementing fire safety procedures, however, they need to be made aware of the following general responsibilities.

- In the event of an emergency, they are required to obey instructions from the Fire Safety Director, Assistant Fire Safety Directors, Fire Warden and local fire personnel.
- To know the locations of all exits, fire alarm manual pull stations and portable fire extinguishers, and the central meeting spot as described in the Fire Safety Plan.
- If a building occupant has a disability that may prevent him/her from using the stairs to evacuate the building, then that person must ensure that he/she is reported on the physical and sensory disabilities list.
- A building occupant is required to report immediately any fire hazards to either the Fire Safety Director, one of the Assistant Fire Safety Directors or the Fire Warden.

EXTINGUISHING, CONTROLLING AND CONFINING A FIRE

Extinguishing, controlling and confining fire is primarily the responsibility of the fire department, however, only after ensuring that the fire alarm has been activated, and the fire department notified, may a person, or persons, familiar with fire extinguishing operations extinguish a small fire.

The key steps in operating a standard portable fire extinguisher are:

1. Release the locking pin from the handle;
2. Approach the fire from the side (never approach a fire directly, or from above it);
3. Direct the extinguishing agent at the base of the fire and proceed in a side to side sweeping motion.

If the fire can not be easily extinguished then the person or persons should leave the fire area immediately, making sure that all doors are closed after leaving.

FIRE HAZARDS

To avoid fire hazards in the building the Assistant Fire Safety Directors, the Fire Warden and the building occupants should be directed:

- To only smoke in designated areas.
- To avoid careless smoking and to always use appropriately designed ashtrays.
- To never dispose of recently light cigarettes or ashes directly into a garbage chute or garbage container.
- To ensure that doors are not kept open by wedges or any other means.
- To turn off and to unplug appliances when not in use.
- To never overload an electrical outlet.
- To never use an unsafe electrical appliance or plug in an electrical device with a frayed or under sized electrical cord.
- To never use exit stairwells or exit corridors as storage areas.
- To never block fire protection equipment, exit corridors or doors.
- To never prop open a fire door.
- To keep the building clean and free of rubbish and other debris.
- To ensure combustible material is not permitted to accumulate in any part of an elevator shaft, ventilating shaft, stairway or other means of egress.
- To ensure that the contents of containers for waste, rubbish and other debris are removed from the building at least once a week.
- To ensure combustible material is not used to absorb flammable and/or combustible liquids.
- To ensure that greasy and oily rags, which are subject to spontaneous heating and/or combustion, are deposited in an appropriate non-combustible receptacle that has been clearly identified for that purpose.
- To ensure that gas barbecues are not used in the building or on balconies.

FIRE EMERGENCY PROCEDURES

The following describe the procedures and responsibilities that are required of the Assistant Fire Safety Directors, Fire Warden and the building occupants during a fire emergency condition.

Duties of Assistant Fire Director 1:

- When a fire alarm is sounded, the Assistant Fire Safety Director 1 will ensure the local fire department is called and that the building elevator has been grounded. The Assistant Fire Safety Director 1 will then proceed to the enunciator panel (located on the ground level in the principal entrance vestibule area) where he/she will acknowledge the alarm signal and obtain all pertinent information associated with the condition of the fire.
- The Assistant Fire Safety Director 1 will ensure that access to the principal door leading onto Start Road is free from any obstruction.
- The Assistant Fire Safety Director 1, or the Assistant Fire Safety Director 2, will immediately notify the Fire Safety Director of the emergency.
- On the arrival of the fire department, the Assistant Fire Safety Director 1 will advise the fire officer in charge of the floor that triggered the alarm and will provide the officer with any other pertinent information that was reported to him/her by Assistant Fire Safety Director 2. A list of persons requiring assistance and all master keys to the building will also be given to the fire officer at this time.
- After the emergency condition is over, and the fire department has declared it safe to re-enter the building, the Fire Safety Director 1 will reset the fire alarm system.

Duties of Assistant Fire Director 2:

- When a fire alarm is sounded the Assistant Fire Safety Director 2 will ensure that the local fire department has been called.
- Immediately after meeting the fire officer in charge, the Assistant Fire Safety Director 2 will provide him/her with a list of tenants under the direct care of the HAPPY PEOPLE.
- The Assistant Fire Safety Director 2 will work in coordination and under the command of the Assistant Fire Safety Director 1.

Duties of Building Occupants:

- Building occupants are required to cooperate with all members of the Fire Safety Committee and with members of the local fire department.
- All ambulatory persons, if able to do so, should remain in their apartments/suites. If this is not a viable option then they should relocate to the closest exit stair and wait for assistance.

Detailed guidelines for building occupants, including occupants with physical and sensory disabilities, are included in Appendix C of the Fire Safety Plan.

FIRE DRILLS

The primary purpose of a fire drill is to ensure that the occupants of the building are familiar with emergency evacuation procedures. The more familiar occupants are the more orderly the evacuation will be.

Advanced notice of a fire drill should be prominently posted. The notice should inform occupants of the date and time of the drill. As a courtesy, the local fire department should also be notified.

The Assistant Fire Director 1 will announce that a fire drill will be held. The Assistant Fire Director 1 will also be responsible for activating one of the pull stations or detectors and recording the actions of the occupants and staff. The Assistant Fire Director 1 will ensure that the fire alarm system operates as designed and that it is audible in all areas of the building.

Following each drill, the Assistant Fire Directors and the Fire Warden will conduct a debriefing, reporting their observations. The results of each drill will be recorded. Fire drills must be conducted in accordance with the Fire Code.

FOR THIS BUILDING THE STATE OF *(include appropriate state)*, FIRE CODE *(include appropriate article)*, REQUIRES THAT DRILLS BE CONDUCTED EVERY *(include appropriate time period)*.

Section IV

PROPOSAL CALL FOR EXTERNAL AUDIT SERVICES

INTRODUCTION TO PROPOSAL CALL FOR EXTERNAL AUDIT SERVICES

The key to selecting an audit firm is a clear understanding of who will do the audit. The experience, competence and the integrity of the firm and the individual staff who will actually do the work is the most important consideration.

In evaluating the competence of an audit firm, attention should be paid to its reputation in the business community, supplemented by private conversations with its current and past clients. Established members of the Board, local associations and friends of the organization can often be very helpful in this kind of reference check.

If the organization is having a good experience with its auditor and is satisfied with the audit cost, then arguments to continue the relationship are obvious. At the same time, a relationship with an auditor that becomes too comfortable may jeopardize the objectivity of the audit. This is why in some jurisdictions, changing auditors periodically is a legal requirement.

Helpful Hints:

- The Board of Directors is the final governing body of the organization. It is therefore responsible for its financial well being. To ensure that this responsibility is satisfied, the Board must be involved in all aspects of the audit, including selecting the audit firm.
- In large organizations, the Board usually appoints an audit committee. The oversight of this committee extends not only to the external audit, but also to internal audits, internal financial controls and external reporting. In medium and small organizations the audit committee may consist of a single Board Director, who because of his/her financial expertise, can take the lead role in satisfying the Board's responsibility.
- The organization should begin the bid out process for an external audit firm by determining the scope of the work, which will form the terms of reference for the engagement. The terms should be prepared by, or be under the close supervision of, the audit committee.
- The full Board of Directors should approve the engagement's terms of reference.
- When the organization is not required to bid out the audit, then the audit committee or the full Board of Directors must use their best judgment and decide when bidding out best serves the interests of the organization.

PROPOSAL CALL FOR EXTERNAL AUDIT SERVICES

Purpose: To solicit bids from external auditing firms who can efficiently and effectively conduct year end audits for The Happy People's: (a) General Operations, and (b) Social Housing Program - Happy Villa.

This document is organized into the following primary sections:

1. OVERVIEW OF THE ORGANIZATION

The Happy People is a community-based non-profit charitable organization that provides attendant services to individuals living with physical disabilities. It is funded through the *(enter appropriate funding sources)* with an annual budget of $1.8 million and currently employs 71 full and part-time staff.

The Happy People also provides recreational and therapeutic programs to adults with physical disabilities in Muppet Land and the surrounding area, through funding provided by the United Way and from donations collected from its own fundraising efforts.

In addition, The Happy People is a non-profit housing provider funded by *(enter appropriate funding sources)*. The Happy People own a 75 unit social housing facility at 456 Start Road in Muppet Land. This project (Happy Villa) currently has an annual budget of $1.5 million and is comprised of both rent geared to income (RGI) and market rent units.

Its fiscal year begins April 1 and ends March 31.

A volunteer Board is responsible for the operation of both the attendant services program and the non-profit housing project. The Annual General Meeting for The Happy People is held in mid-June.

2. TENDERING PROCESS

2.1 Closing Date and Time

Two sealed and completed copies of the proposal must be received and time stamped no later than *(enter appropriate time and date)* at The Happy People office, 456 Start Road, Muppet Land, *(enter appropriate provincial and Postal code)*. Address your envelope to the attention of the Executive Director *(enter appropriate name)*.

Late bids will be returned unopened.

2.2 Enquiries

Enquiries regarding the process and the format of your return should be directed to the Executive Director, The Happy People, at *(enter appropriate telephone, fax and or email address).*

2.3 Changes

Verbal clarification should not be interpreted as a change of intent, content or scope of the request for proposal.

Any revision to the request for proposal will be issued as addenda that will be acknowledged within your submission.

2.4 Briefing Session

Those submitting a proposal are invited to attend a briefing information session at The Happy People office, on *(enter appropriate day and time).*

2.5 Interviews

Short listed candidates may be asked to attend an interview with staff and/or designated Board members before the final selection is made. These candidates will be contacted by telephone on or before *(enter appropriate date)* to schedule this meeting.

2.6 Decision

The selection and appointment of the successful firm will be confirmed at the Annual General Meeting in June 20xx. The appointment will take effect for the 20xx/20xx fiscal year (year end March 31, 20xx).

3. ELIGIBILITY

Before preparing your response, candidates are advised to ensure that their firm meets the following set of eligibility criteria. The firm has:

(a) experience in providing similar audit services to other non-profit groups;
(b) well-developed professional auditing techniques and a sound system of control and review of audit work performed;
(c) adequate resources and support services available to adequately complete the task;
(d) experienced, well-qualified staff who can work on the audit consistently from one year to the next; and
(e) the available staff and support services to complete the engagement during April and May.

4. SCOPE AND REQUIREMENTS

4.1 General

The audit will be comprised of the following two sections:
- The Happy People - General Operations
- The Happy People - Social Housing Program

Each section of the audit will be conducted simultaneously but will result in separate sets of financial statements.

Commencing with the 20xx/20xx fiscal year, the audit for The Happy People - General Operations will include:

(a) examination of the records and financial statements;
(b) preparation of an audit report to the President and members of the Board; and
(c) a report to funding sources, *(enter appropriate funding sources)*, in the prescribed form. This report is to be completed subsequent to a Board review of the financial information contained in the organization's Annual Information Return.

Commencing with the 20xx/20xx fiscal year, the audit for The Happy People – Social Housing Program will include:

(a) at least one on-site visit to the office of the property management company;
(b) examination of the records and financial statements;
(c) preparation of an audit report to the President and members of the Board;
(d) preparation of the Annual Information Return as required by the funding agency; and
(e) assistance with all Provincial and Federal tax rebate applications, where appropriate.

For both sections of the audit, the auditor's work will not include accounting with the exception of year end adjusting and closing entries resulting from the audit. However, physical preparation of financial statements for each section of the audit and/or schedules is required (as shown in attachments).

4.2 Annual Schedule

At least one month prior to each year end (the fiscal year ends March 31), the auditor will meet with designated staff of the organization to discuss and agree upon a schedule for the completion of work for the current year. The schedule for completion will detail the hours required by the audit firm broken down by staff level.

The auditor will maintain a record of time spent on each task and submit it to the designated staff member upon the completion of the audit, along with a schedule comparing actual with budgeted results and explanations of significant variances between the two. The cost of this requirement will be considered to be included in the fees quoted under this proposal.

4.3 Qualified Statements

Immediately upon discovery of information or conditions that will lead to the inclusion of a qualified opinion (other than current qualifications) with respect to any of the organization's financial statements, the auditor will inform and fully discuss such matters with the designated staff member. Also, the auditor will, as far as possible, allow a reasonable amount time for The Happy People to investigate, analyze, and take such corrective action as to avoid the inclusion of such an opinion.

4.4 Meeting and Subsequent Assistance

The auditor will attend such meetings as are called to discuss their work and reports, and will provide such information as requested, to enhance the understanding of the Board members concerning matters pertaining to the annual financial statements.

The auditor will be available to meet at least twice in the course of the audit year with a designated staff member, the finance committee and/or Board of Directors to discuss matters of mutual concern. Senior audit staff will also make themselves available to attend the Annual General Meeting.

The cost of any additional meetings beyond those outlined above should be itemized separately as part of the quote.

4.5 Post-Audit Management Letter

No later than fifteen working days following the completion of annual statements the auditor will prepare and deliver draft letters, to the office of The Happy People, conveying any concerns that may have been discovered. The auditor will also provide recommendations on how to remedy these concerns.

Not less then ten working days prior to the Annual General meeting, the auditor will also meet with designated representatives of the organization, at which time, appropriate responses to these audit concerns will be discussed.

Adherence to the critical dates and requirements outlined within this proposal call and the annual schedule will be an essential feature of satisfactory performance under this engagement.

4.6 Terms of Engagement

It is expected that the successful firm will be the auditor for The Happy People for a period of five years beginning at the 20xx/20xx fiscal year end. However, the appointment will be on an annual basis at the Annual General Meeting for a term of one year and the Board reserves the right to not reappoint if dissatisfied in any way with performance, fees charged, or any other elements of the service provided.

5. PROPOSAL CONTENT

The proposal must be structured to provide the following information:

- a profile of the firm, including breadth of other audit assignments/clients, identification of the partner responsible for the audit, resource and support services available, and particular strengths relevant to the audit;
- experience of the firm in non-profit housing and social services auditing;
- familiarity with the client's accounting software *(enter accounting software used)*;
- a description of the auditing techniques to be utilized and procedures for reviewing the audit work and the financial statements;
- the location of the office responsible for the audit, the names of the partner(s), manager(s), and senior staff who will be assigned to the audit if the firm is successful **(continuity of staff will be given a high priority and ability to achieve this must be so indicated in the proposal);**
- the names and contact information of client officials for three of the firm's present audits who would act as contact references, at least one of which must be a non-profit housing provider;
- an estimate of the number of hours that will be required for the annual audit, broken down by level of staff assigned to each major section;
- fees and expenses in a format as described under Section 6 below;
- commitment to the terms and conditions of the proposal call;
- information regarding any advisory services which may be available to The Happy People free of charge, including, but not limited to, publications dealing with matters such as Provincial and Federal tax rebate applications, income tax, internal audit, financial systems development and cash management; and
- an explanation of why your firm should be the successful candidate under the proposal. Information on this item must be specific, detailed and verifiable.

6. FEES AND EXPENSES

The proposal must include a firm quotation for the fees to be charged for the 20xx/20xx audit (itemizing each section of the audit) and an estimate of fees for the remaining four years. Details will be provided as to the number of hours required, broken down by staff level and the hourly rate being charged for each. Fees should be quoted separately for each section of the audit (listed below) and based on the specifications as outlined in Appendices A & B:

- The Happy People - General Operations
- The Happy People - Social Housing Program

Out-of-pocket expenses should be clearly stated to be either part of the estimated fee or shown separately.

If less time is required to perform the audit than anticipated, it is expected that a fee reduction will be given.

An indication should be given in the proposal as to how fees for work outside the scope of this proposal will be determined.

7. SUBMISSION

Candidates will reply to the proposal in sufficient detail to provide a basis for evaluation. Appendices A & B are provided as sample formats to ensure that a standardized level of information is submitted.

Candidates may be required to provide additional information or clarification on the contents of their submissions or may be required to confirm statements on capacity or cost.

Proposals that fail to provide the required information or are incomplete or obscure, or which contain erasures, alterations or irregularities, may be rejected.

8. CONDITIONS

The Happy People reserves the right to discuss any and all proposals, to request additional information from those submitting a proposal, and to decline any and all proposals made. The lowest cost proposal will not necessarily be accepted.

The Happy People will not be liable for any costs incurred in the preparation of a response to this proposal.

9. SELECTION CRITERIA

Selection criteria will include, but not be limited to the:

- experience of the firm in the auditing of non-profit housing and/or other social services;
- experience of the personnel assigned to the audit;
- quality of the proposal and presentation and compliance with proposal call requirements;
- auditor's statement of understanding of the overall scope of work;
- references; and
- fees.

10. MONITORING AUDITOR PERFORMANCE

10.1 Adherence to Proposed Fee

It is expected that the successful candidate keep to the annual fees quoted.

10.2 Persons assigned to the Audit

For the initial year of the engagement, the persons assigned to the audit should be those originally proposed. Subsequent changes should be limited. It is expected that senior audit staff will be present throughout much of the audit and that the partner would be available to attend regular meetings, as outlined in Section 4.4 of this proposal call.

10.3 Conditions and Deadlines

It is expected that the audit will be carried out in the manner proposed. It is also expected that the audit will be completed within the time frame specified in this proposal call, and any other targets for completion will be met on a timely basis.

11. SCHEDULE OF ATTACHMENTS

- Appendix A
- Appendix B
- The Happy People – General Operations (*attach full set of most recent audited statements)*
- The Happy People – Social Housing Program (*attach full set of most recent audited statements)*

APPENDIX A

SPECIFICATIONS AND PRICING

ORGANIZATION: The Happy People - General Operations

NUMBER OF PROGRAM SITES: 3

FUNDING PROGRAM(S): *(enter appropriate funding sources).*

COMPUTER ACCOUNTING PROGRAM: *(enter appropriate accounting software).*

AUDIT REQUIREMENTS:

i Examination of the records and financial statements;
ii Preparation of an audit report to the President and members of the Board;
iii Report to the funding agency *(enter appropriate funding sources)* in the prescribed form. This report is to be completed subsequent to a Board review of the financial statements contained in the corporation's Annual Information Return.

YEAR END: March 31

Year 20aa/20bb Audit Fees		
Staff Level	Hourly Rate	Estimate of Hours
1.	$	
2.	$	
3.	$	
4.	$	
Out-of-pocket expenses	Included	$
Hourly rate for additional work		

ESTIMATES

20bb/20cc	$	20cc/20dd	$	200dd/20ee	$	20ee/20/ff	$

APPENDIX B

SPECIFICATIONS AND PRICING

ORGANIZATION: The Happy People - Social Housing Program (Happy Villa)

UNITS UNDER MANAGEMENT: 75

NUMBER OF BUILDINGS/SITES: 1

FUNDING PROGRAM(S): *(enter appropriate funding sources).*

COMPUTER ACCOUNTING PROGRAM: *(enter appropriate accounting software).*

AUDIT REQUIREMENTS:

i On-site visit to office of the property management company;
ii Examination of the records and financial statements;
iii Preparation of an audit report to the President and members of the Board;
iv Preparation of the Annual Information Return;
v Assistance with all Provincial and Federal tax rebate applications, where appropriate.

YEAR END: March 31

Year 20aa/bb Audit Fees			
Staff Level	Hourly Rate		Estimate of Hours
1.	$		
2.	$		
3.	$		
4.	$		
Out-of-pocket expenses	Included		$
Hourly rate for additional work			

ESTIMATES

20bb/20cc	$	20cc/20dd	$	20dd/20ee	$	20ee/20ff	$

Section V

THE NON-PROFIT BOARD OF DIRECTORS

INTRODUCTION TO THE NON-PROFIT BOARD OF DIRECTORS

The Board of Directors acts as the final authority for non-profit organizations. The primary function of the Board is oversight (i.e., creating, defining and enforcing policies and procedures of accountability that enable the organization's executive management to carryout their duties efficiently, and in the best interests of its stakeholders). In order for this to happen, the Board must work collaboratively with management.

Candidates for election to the Board are selected for their character, acumen, and in some cases for their expertise in specific areas. It is each member's responsibility to spend the necessary time to discharge their responsibilities in a professional way.

The Board also has a responsibility to renew itself. It does this by electing new members as the terms of old members expire. The continuation on the Board of each member should be reviewed at the expiration of the member's term in office.

Being asked to sit as a Director on a non-profit Board is both an honor and a great responsibility.

Helpful Hints:

- A good Board of Directors is introspective and forward thinking. It plans for the future needs of the organization, and ensures that there will be a generous overlap in members who will fill key Board positions.

- A formal agenda needs to be sent out well in advance of Board or Committee meetings. This allows participants to prepare for the meeting and make the most efficient use of their time. An agenda also helps to ensure that participants will stay on track. Consequently, meetings are more focused and more ground is covered.

- At the start of a meeting, the Chair should ask if there are any additions to the prepared agenda. The Chair should move through the agenda and keep the discussion focused, ensuring that each item is discussed thoroughly before moving onto the next one. The minutes resulting from a meeting need to be prepared and distributed to the participants as soon as possible.

- With so many non-profit organizations looking for volunteers, it is important to make the Director's position as interesting and as fulfilling as possible. A simple thank you note for a job well done or mailing out a birthday card is an inexpensive way to show a volunteer member of the organization that he/she is appreciated.

THE NON-PROFIT BOARD OF DIRECTORS

Most non-profit charitable organizations have Boards of Directors. This document discusses the Roles and Responsibilities of Boards and the relationship they have with the organizations they serve.

This document is organized into the following primary sections:

1. REASONS FOR A BOARD OF DIRECTORS

There are three principal reasons why organizations have Boards of Directors. These include a legal reason, an administrative reason and a supervisory reason.

The Legal Reason: State law governs how an organization will be incorporated and how it will be structured. Incorporation legitimizes the corporation and thereby adds to its stability. Incorporation also provides Directors and Officers of the organization with limited protection from civil liability.

The most important feature for non-profit organizations, however, is that it may secure a US Treasury Department exemption.

The Administrative Reason: The Executive Director, also known as the Chief Executive Officer, is the head of operations in an organization. Because of the power this position holds, it needs to be closely monitored and administered. This is the function of the Board of Directors.

The Supervisory Reason: Non-profit Boards exist to ensure that the best interests of their organization's constituents are met. Boards are also there to ensure that established policies and procedures are followed, and that when a change in direction is required existing policies and procedures are appropriately changed and approved.

Like the Boards of for-profit organizations, non-profit Boards are also there to protect and manage the assets and liabilities of the organization they serve.

2. EXPECTATIONS FROM THE BOARD

The Board of Directors is the essence of the organization.

Members of the Board must be willing to lend their individual talents and expertise whenever asked. Board members must also be willing to commit the time necessary to attend Board meetings, participate on committees and attend the many special events run by, or for, the organization.

Boards oversee the operations of the organization and work collaboratively with its executive management. Boards protect and promote the organization's goals and ensure that its constituents are well served. To do this meaningfully, individual Board members must have a good understanding of how the organization works. This understanding comes from knowledge, and the amount of knowledge a member has is determined by the number of hours that a member devotes to doing his/her Board work.

Participating on a non-profit Board can be rewarding. To be of maximum value to the Board, the organization and its constituents, however, a member must be prepared to make a serious time commitment.

3. ROLE AND RESPOSIBILITY OF THE BOARD OF DIRECTORS

Most non-profit and for-profit Boards of Directors share the following basic roles and responsibilities.

3.1 Set the Organization's Long Term Mission

The Board of Directors is responsible for creating, monitoring, and when necessary, updating the organization's mission statement. A mission statement is visionary. It explains why the organization exists, who it serves, and what it hopes to accomplish.

3.2 Create and Implement an Action Plan

The Board of Directors is responsible for creating the organization's strategic plan. Among other things, the strategic plan includes staffing requirements, the programs and services the organization offers, and possible funding sources.

The plan is a collaborative effort with input coming from the Board, management, staff, volunteers, and experts in the organization's area of interest.

3.3 Select the Executive Director

The Board writes and approves the job description for the Executive Director's position. The description should be unambiguous and include clear expectations for the job.

The Board of Directors also hires the Executive Director and establishes the rate of compensation. Conversely, the Board has the responsibility of dismissing the Executive Director when the goals of the organization are consistently not met, or when the Executive Director's conduct is unethical or unbecoming.

3.4 Support and Evaluate the Executive Director

On an ongoing basis the Board of Directors has the responsibility of monitoring and evaluating the performance of the Executive Director. As the Board hires, and if necessary dismisses the Executive Director, monitoring and evaluating performance becomes self-serving.

The Board of Directors must also support their Executive Director. Support is particularly important when tough, and often unpopular decisions, are required to meet the organization's goals.

3.5 Maintain and Revitalize the Board

The Board of Directors is responsible for maintaining its own well being. It needs to develop and grow along with the organization. The Board must ensure that members who leave are replaced by qualified and committed new members, and that the composition of the Board remains balanced.

Senior Board members must ensure that new members are well oriented and trained, and that there is continuity in the Board.

3.6 Encourage and Develop Strong Public Support

Non-profit organizations exist to serve their constituents. Donations and grants from municipal, state, and federal governments are their chief source of funds. The Board has a responsibility to increase these funds so that current services can be expanded and new programs can be added. This is accomplished by promoting a positive united vision of the organization and by lobbying grant funding sources.

The Board should be an organization's biggest fund raiser.

3.7 Safeguard and Effectively Manage Resources

The Board of Directors oversees the resource management of the organization and ensures that they are used efficiently and effectively, and for the purposes intended. The Board also hires and evaluates the organization's external auditors, and considers whether to implement or ignore the recommendations that result from the audit.

The Board helps develop annual budgets, and during the year, monitors actual revenues and expenditures with budget projections. All budgets should be approved by the Board.

3.8 Safeguard the Organization's Integrity and Accountability

The Board of Directors is the organization's final authority. The Board creates and approves all by-laws and policies and, on an ongoing basis, monitors the actions of the organization to ensure that they are followed.

4. ROLE AND RESPONSIBILITY OF A BOARD MEMBER

Each member of the Board of Directors exists to serve the organization and to help ensure that its mission is being fulfilled. Each member is responsible to see that the policies of the organization are adhered to and that its resources are being spent wisely.

Directors must learn to act as a team. A Director should not take action on his/her own when group action is called for. A single Board member who does take action without the approval of the entire Board can, indeed, cause the organization serious harm.

Directors must be prepared to:

- attend all, or a large majority, of Board meetings;
- help create policies that will improve, protect, and help the organization grow;
- serve on, or act as the Chair for standing committees, subcommittees and working groups;
- promote the programs and services of the organization whenever possible; and
- actively participate in panels, workshops and any other activity that will benefit the organization.

Once elected, each member of the Board becomes an ambassador for the organization.

5. COMMON BOARD COMMITTEES

In addition to attending and participating in Board meetings, each Director must be willing to participate in at least one committee. The committees reported below are the most common ones found in today's non-profit business environment:

Executive: Acts as the final authority of the organization, subject only to the Board of Directors.
The Executive Committee most often consists of a Chairperson, a Vice-chair, past Chair of the Executive Committee, the Treasurer, and the Executive Director of the organization. The Executive Director's position on the Executive Committee is a non voting position and is there only as a resource person.

In most organizations, members of the Executive Committee are obliged to maintain a good set of records so that they can be passed on to their successors.

Building and Grounds: Develop and implement a facility's maintenance plan so that a safe and comfortable environment can be enjoyed by staff, visitors, and service consumers.

Development: Increase the organization's donor base so that current and future financial needs will be met. Collaborate with the Finance Committee to develop and maintain an endowment fund that can provide the organization with a guaranteed steady stream of future revenues.

Finance: Oversee the financial management of the organization, including its budgeting and investing functions, and provide the Board of Directors with regular oral and written financial updates.

Membership: Ensure that there is always a good cross section of eligible Board members who can provide the organization with their expertise when required. Develop and operate an orientation program for newly elected members.
Personnel: Review, evaluate and keep personnel policies and related matters current and in compliance with state and federal labor laws. Develop the Executive Director's compensation package for Board discussion and approval.

Program and Planning: Monitor, evaluate and when possible improve current programs and how they are delivered. In collaboration with the Executive Director, develop a strategic plan that will assist the organization meet its mission and surpass its goals.

Promotion and Public Relations: Increase the visibility of the organization and promote its programs and its services. The actions of this committee have a huge impact on all other committees, particularly Finance and Membership.

6. CONFLICT OF INTEREST

Members of the Board should not directly or indirectly gain, or appear to gain, any financial advantage from the relationship that membership brings. It is essential that Directors always act in the best interest of the organization.

The first agenda item at all Board meetings should be a call for a declaration of conflict of interest. If a conflict of interest is declared, then the member declaring the conflict should not attend that part of the meeting that contains the conflict, and should note vote on the matter if a motion is put forward.

7. DIRECTOR INDEMNIFICATION

The organization must ensure that each Director is indemnified against all expenses and liabilities, including counsel fees, except where the Director is found guilty of willful misfeasance or misfeasance in the performance of his/her duties.

Appropriate indemnification of a Director is an important selling point when recruiting new members.

Thank you for purchasing:

Financial and Administrative Policies and Procedures and Other Essentials for the Not-For-Profit Organization – 4th Edition

As a token of our appreciation, we would like to provide you with a soft copy of our manual in order to facilitate the incorporation of its content into your organization's Policies and Procedures.

Please visit our website at: **http://www.SiliconSurfers.com/PubPlus** and complete the request form so that we can email your copy of the manual in Microsoft Word (2003 version) format.

Please keep in mind that this file is provided to you as a courtesy. Please respect our copyright and only make such copies as are required by **your organization alone**.

Sincerely,

Gary J. Scapinello, BA, CMA
President, Publications Plus

Breinigsville, PA USA
22 December 2009

229697BV00001B/9/A